The Five Minute Failure

"The light-hearted look at success in work and life"

Beginner failure
the route to self-destruction

Intermediate failure
taking the office and your team to pieces

Advanced failure
get into, and bring down the entire organisation

First published in Great Britain in March 2006 by Rock Publishing

Rock-Hill Publishing
Central House
4 Roborough Walk
Hornchurch
Essex
RM12 6QJ

© Kevin McAlpin and Michael Millar 2006

Kevin McAlpin and Michael Millar assert their moral rights to be identified as the authors of this work.

A catalogue record for this book is available from the British Library

ISBN: 0-9552588-0-4

Illustrations by Tony Healey www.th-illustration.co.uk

College of Failure crest designed by Kyle Hermans

Typeset, printed and bound in the UK by Digisource GB Ltd., Livingston

All rights reserved. No part of this publication may be reproduced, stored in a retrieval system, or transmitted, in any form or by any means electronic, mechanical, photocopying, recording or otherwise, without prior permission of the publishers.

Every effort has been made to trace copyright owners. Please notify Rock Publishing of any omissions and they will be rectified.

Without whom this book would never have been written:

Kevin would like to thank:

Mum, Dad for a great start in life, my wife Victoria and children, Nicholas, Anneliese and Olivia for supporting me to balance work, directing a business, being chairman of a charity, constantly learning and reading with playing sport, keeping fit and writing books and a great family life. Martin Pretlove for the support to start Performance Coaching International (PCI) all those years ago. Louise Bradshaw, Andrew Daley, Dawn Wilkinson and Christopher Hirst for their constant feedback, advice and opinions which helped to develop my thoughts and the Five Minute Failure concept. All the coaches from PCI especially Sue White, Gary Bean, Ann Kennedy, John Van Maurik and Tammy Tawadros for their questions and insights. Finally the 1000s of people I have interviewed, spoken to, questioned, spoken at their conferences, coached and socialised with from the rich and famous to more importantly the normal woman/man in the street who aligned happiness and success. Finally to all the authors who have inspired me to take action and write this book.

Michael would like to thank:

Mum, Dad, Clive, Alan, Jennifer and all his family for giving him everything a person could ask for. He would also like to thank his long-suffering friends, beautiful girlfriend Susanna and colleagues for indulging his whims and flights of fancy over the years. He would also like to thank all the public and private figures without whose successes and disasters he couldn't do his job.

Finally we would like to say a big thank you to Tony Healey probably in our opinion the best rugby flyhalf never to be capped by Wales at rugby union for the illustrations throughout the book.

Why should you pay any attention to these guys?

Kevin McAlpin

Kevin is regarded by many as one of the UK's leading Executive Performance Coaches. A professional speaker who was originally a highly successful Sales and Operational manager, Kevin has held various HR board level roles within the financial services sector. As managing director of Performance Coaching International, he is a Leadership development specialist delivering one-on-one and group sessions to senior executives from major companies in the UK, Europe and the US. He has won many business awards by way of recognition for his innovative business focused coaching and development strategies including an Individual National Training Award. He was also a finalist in HR Manager of the Year run by the Personnel Today magazine. His qualifications include a MSC in HR Consultancy and another in International HRM. A certified Trainer of NLP. He is currently studying for a Phd in Performance Coaching.

Renowned as an expert in decision making, Kevin is the author of various published articles and co-author of the forthcoming book entitled "Coach the Executive Coach" by Kogan Page.

Kevin's keen interest in sports led him into coaching athletes where success at the top level is as much in the mind as the skills. He has coached International Sports people from a wide range of sports including Olympic, world and European record holders. He has also previously been the official PGA EURO PRO Golf Tour performance coach.

Michael Millar

Michael is a journalist specialising in employment and industrial relations. He has interviewed some of the UK's leading businessmen, politicians, and unionists and witnessed firsthand some of the great successes and catastrophic failures they have orchestrated.

Michael was the first business journalist to visit Iraq following the end of the second Gulf war. He returned again in February 2006 to investigate the impact of the Territorial Army on the war in Iraq armed only with the question: 'Shouldn't you be at your desk?'

He was awarded the title 'News Writer of the Year 2005' for his pains.

In his time as a journalist Michael has covered the sublime and the ridiculous – from Whitehall wranglings over issues of national concern, such as the UK's looming pensions crisis to the multi-million pound items of jewellery and perfume that bedeck the rich and famous.

He has travelled widely from the highways of America to the jungles of Papua New Guinea.

Michael holds a degree in Law from the University of East Anglia and an MA in International Business and Management from the University of Westminster. He has a post-graduate diploma in journalism from the London School of Journalism and is a Fellow of the Royal Society for the Encouragement of Arts, Manufactures and Commerce.

He also plays the guitar and sings in a rock band called Meerkat Population Explosion.

What is this book about and why should you read it?

This book is about how to succeed in work and life. It is based on two very simple principles. The first is that you can learn just as much from failure as you can from success. Acts of failure tend to make great examples of what needs to be done, or avoided, to succeed, just as much as acts of success do. If you ignore either side of the coin, you'll never be more than half way there.

The second principle is, no one ever said learning had to be dull. There is no better way to discover and commit information to memory than through entertainment. This is why you remember last night's episode of the soap opera but none of this morning's meeting. Knowledge is power, but it need not be rocket science.

This is why we have created the College of Failure and its venerable professors who will do their damnest to lead you on the road to wrack and ruin. It is an extra formula for pointing out what experts of failure would do as well as those who are on the way to glory. It is as fun as it is effective to learn in this way.

Your professors are a coach and journalist respectively; professions which have given them access to some of the most powerful and successful people in the world. As an executive and performance coach in the realms of both corporate and sporting success, Kevin has met and coached some of the highest performing individuals on God's green earth. He has worked with clients with all sorts of aims and goals; some want to make the company succeed, others want to win an Olympic gold or beat a world record.

He also invested many years in attending training courses and workshops, watching the good, the bad and the ugly speak at conferences and listening to audio tapes on those long journeys in the car.

Michael has spent his career bothering politicians, businessmen and trade unionists and when not actually talking to them, holding a magnifying glass up to their behaviour. He is still constantly amazed at what a mess some of these people can make of things despite their intellect, training and experience.

One thing they have noticed over all this time is that successful individuals are generally all exceptionally resilient. They all bounce back quickly from setbacks and failures. Often the greatest reasons for their success were the lessons they learned from their failures.

> *"Accept failure as a normal part of living; make a note of its lessons and move on"*
>
> Tom Hobson – *musician*

Kevin and Michael also realised that all the motivational talks, books, tapes and courses had been focusing on the 'Can do'/ 'American Dream'/ 'no such thing as failure' mind set. These are all valuable if people take the knowledge, couple it with the appropriate action and make it part of their day-to-day routine.

But more often than not these books or talks do not work for people. You will read it (or start to read it), you will learn the theory, but you won't put it into practice. At the end of the day you just get bogged down with chasing what can seem an impossible dream.

And it's not your fault

It is the inevitable result of being faced with a mountain of complicated things to think about while you're already rushed off your feet in daily life anyway.

You see, it's all very well knowing the theory, but presenting it in a way that people actually can digest is an entirely different matter altogether. Most books on success get far too wrapped up in how clever they are to really care whether the masses can actually understand them. A recent survey of over 300 HR directors found:

- Over 85% had purchased a book on success or personal development
- One in six (16%) left the book(s) on the shelf totally unread
- Almost all of them (83%) said they had read the book and then never put the learning into action.

If Marx was right in saying religion is the opiate of the masses, then more often than not success books are the prescription strength sleeping pills of the masses.

For this reason, this could be the first ever book about how to succeed in life and in business that is actually fun to read.

This book offers short, sharp principles and rules you need to get ahead and that can be incorporated into daily life with minimal hassle. It addresses both what to do and what not to do in your quest for success and it unashamedly does this in a light-hearted way. It is a book that can actually be incorporated into daily life without making it a chore. We hope to see people reading it on the beach.

It avoids the two things that are guaranteed to put you off the quest for self-improvement – reams of impenetrable information and stultifying tedium.

Instead this book is designed for people to have fun and learn from others who have got things wrong as well as right. This allows you to reflect on your own situation, making you aware of what you might need to stop doing. It will also point out what you need to keep doing and a number of things you need to start doing.

We have included short summaries of each lesson in the form of 'success warnings' at the end of each lesson to leave you with a clear message of just what it takes to succeed.

Remember that with just a little knowledge about how to get ahead, you will automatically rise above the majority of the population. We have seen it more times than we can count.

Good luck!

Yours,

Michael Millar and *Kevin McAlpin*
May 2006

CONTENTS PAGE

 INDUCTION TO THE COLLEGE OF FAILURE   17

 Section One – Beginner Failure   25
Personal failure

The Curriculum:

Start as you mean to go on
    setting up your day for maximum failure   27
Always look on the dark side of life
    thinking positively   29
Being a shrinking violet
    how to hide in the background   31
Simply the best – better than all the rest
    avoiding humility   33
Effort is too much like hard work
    amount of endeavour = amount of success   35
Money, money, money, it's not funny
    making work a burden   36
Just say yes!
    prioritising your tasks   38
In the zone
    how not to take risks   40
Fear factor
    why there's not much to worry about   42
Best laid plans
    why planning leads to success   44
Omniscience is a virtue
    the importance of learning   45
Laxtion man
    seizing opportunity   46
Hat-trick
    having meaningful goals   47

Low fidelity
   believing in yourself   49
Added value failure
   what is important to you?   52
Mirror, mirror on the wall
   putting things in perspective   53
Do worry, don't be happy
   happiness = success   57
Knowledge is sour
   pinpointing what worries you   58
Honesty is the worst policy
   the art of self-denial   59
Beg, borrow and steal, steal, steal
   giving office property a new home   61
Handling rejection
   how you can learn from being put down   63
A measure of success
   hitting your targets   65
Keeping a wobbly upper lip
   the importance of emotion   65
Relationships – failure has a partner
   the six keys to a successful relationship   67

Section Two – Intermediate Failure
Workplace and team-based failure   79

The Curriculum:

Cultural awareness
   understanding the work environment   81
Schoolyard politics
   having the courage of your convictions   82
Them and us
   working with management   83
Woof! Meouw!
   learning to say no   85
Hard times
   having long-term vision   87

We need a volunteer	
when to put your hand up	88
In for a penny	
when to put your hand down	89
Reading the small print	
under-promise and over-deliver	90
Tip the work-life balance	
work smarter not harder	92
Client shmi-ent	
establish the needs of the ones who count	93
The apparel oft proclaims the man	
looking the part	94
Feel the pain of branding	
creating your personal profile	96
Questions, questions, questions	
the only way to get an answer	97
Mentor? Mental, more like!	
finding someone to lead you	98
***Fist* impressions last**	
getting off on the right foot	99
Failure: a team game for all ages	
what does a high-performing team look like?	102
Relationships on the sea of failure	
successful networking	105
A word in their ears	
understanding what others think	106
"You expect me to talk?"	
keeping confidential information under raps	108
It's good to talk	
humans were meant to speak face-to-face	109
Lies, damned lies and statistics	
don't hide mistakes	111
Gossip is great – or so we have been told	
if you don't have anything nice to say…	113
Telling it like it is	
don't mince words	115
Practise makes perfect	
perfecting your skills	116

Feeding yourself backwards
    listening to good advice   117
Letting it all out
    telling people just what you think   120
Making a positive into a negative
    the outlook is bright   121

Section Three – Advanced Failure
Getting into and bringing down the organisation   125

The Curriculum:

It's lonely at the top
    what facets do great leaders have?   127
Thanks for the memories
    how to improve your memory   128
Mr Demotivator
    treating individuals as individuals   131
The wrong words at the wrong time
    thinking before you speak   132
The ethical dilemma
    making the right and decent decisions   133
Never a kind word
    saying your Ps & Qs   136
A quiet word in your ear...
    being downright rude   137
We are now a part of the tribe
    analysing how the company works   140
Judging a book by its cover
    who does what to whom at work?   143
Please lie down on the couch...
    too much love to give   145
Taking a view on an interview
    being prepared for the big day   146
Having the vision to fail
    thinking positively   149

Feel the fear
    overcoming the primeval fight or flight response   151
Mind reading is not an open book
    if you have something to say then say it   152
Throw some darts and see how many stick
    the joy of management buzzwords   154
Speed is of the offence
    more haste – less speed   156

An Epilogue of Sorts   161

A final thought from our sponsors
    the whole book in one page   163
Once upon a time
    a memory aid for you   165
The story of Optimistic   167
A final, final thought from our sponsors   169

APPENDIX ONE
An alphabet for success   173

APPENDIX TWO
How to play buzzword bingo   175

APPENDIX THREE
Chevy Nova Awards   176

Induction to the College of Failure

Welcome to the venerable College of Failure. It is delightful to have you in our care. Please make sure you are sitting uncomfortably and we'll get started on letting you know just how to fail, derail your career and generally make a mess of all and sundry.

You are one of the many thousands of students who have passed through our doors with the sole purpose of deteriorating your wellbeing – and with any luck, the wellbeing of those around you.

But before we go any further, you have to make a decision. Should you read on? There is every chance that if you do you might pick up bad habits that will lead you on to success in one form or other. This is just a hazard of this vocation sadly. To fail comprehensively takes real dedication.

It might be better if you just put this book on the shelf next to the other tomes on leadership, management and financial wellbeing where it will look pretty and sooth the guilt you might feel were you not the proud owner of a vast amount of theory. We used an especially long sentence there because everyone else who writes 'success' books does and we were feeling left out.

Still here? Good. Much of what you read in this book might seem familiar. Now and again you'll look at the wise words contained herein and go 'I don't believe it! That is so obvious!' Of course all the best things are; it just takes some enterprising soul to point them out.

With these glad thoughts in our hearts we are ready to begin a journey that will take us through the finest virtues a human being can possess – ignorance, arrogance, fear and of course a smattering of good old bigotry.

This book will hopefully change your life. Yes, we're thinking big! We like to think it's as important as the Dead Sea Scrolls, except it's more like the Dead End Scrolls.

So a toast! To making a success of failure, or if you'd rather, to making a failure of success.

Not-so humbly yours,

The Professors of the College of Failure

THE INDUCTION

Here's a test for you to see just what stage you're at in the failure stakes.

The College of Failure Success Questionnaire

Find out your success rating by completing the following questionnaire, reflecting on the last 12 months

5   Very typical of the way I am/act

4   Frequently typical of the way I am/act

3   Sometimes typical of the way I am/act

2   Seldom typical of the way I am/act

1   Never typical of the way I am/act

I gain visibility for my work	
I am optimistic in attitude	
I react to setbacks by bouncing back and trying harder	
I set SMART goals that are realistic and time bound	
I trust myself to take calculated risks	
I am clear about the reasons why people select me above others to carry out tasks	
I find it easy to turn situations to my advantage	
I am proactive; I do not wait for opportunities. I go out and look for them	
I regularly plan	
I regularly look for opportunities to develop my skills	
I set stretching targets	
I seek to stop, reflect and learn when I fail to reach targets	
I make sure that my message gets across and is understood	
I eat a healthy breakfast within an hour of waking	
I conform to the dress code at work	

People would say I have humility	
I feel confident inside and project that to others	
I endeavour to work hard	
Work is never a burden to me	
I totally motivate myself	
I work to overcome my fears	
I focus on my current job as if it is the last, whilst always asking: "is this improving my career prospects?"	
I look at everything as an opportunity to learn	
I put my skills and knowledge to good use	
I regularly celebrate success	
I feel challenged and stretched at work	
I am resilient	
I quickly adapt to circumstances	
I believe in myself	
I believe as much can be learnt from failure as success	
I am inspired by my goals	
I am self-aware and continually look for ways to improve my self-awareness	
I am honest with myself	
I embrace my emotions and do not suppress them	
I talk openly and honestly	
I can keep a secret or confidence	
I have the courage of my convictions	
I set clear boundaries of what I will and will not do; what I will and will not accept	
I have a successful work life balance	
I volunteer for things strategically	
I put time and effort into building trust relationships	
I go the extra mile for my clients	
I am focused	
I am inquisitive	

I ask questions to confirm understanding	
I have a mentor or coach or trusted friend	
I regularly seek advice	
I have a firm handshake	
I pay attention to others and their needs	
I analyse and evaluate situations	
I nurture my talents and practice, practice, practice	
I seek to get feedback from others regardless of whether it is good or bad?	
I am flexible and adaptable	
I can motivate others	
I see situations from multiple views and perspectives	
I can control my emotions	
I regularly analyse my environment	
I network well	
I have a positive mental attitude	
I play to my strengths	
I put my decisions into action	
I trust others	
I consider myself lucky	
I have common sense	
I am the person that I always wanted to be	
I care about others	
I still dream about things	
I care about my reputation	
I go out and look for inspiration	
I am open to new ideas?	
I have a check list and action plan with milestones towards my goals and visions	
I have a good posture	
I feel in control	
I feel happy	

I deal with issues as and when they arise	
I can handle rejection	
I am committed	
I communicate well, listening, asking, questioning and summarising as well as talking	
I have a good network of people	
I am ethical	
I always prepare properly where possible	
As appropriate, I will challenge and speak out	
I seek to stop, reflect and learn when I have successes or reach targets	
I have a healthy balanced diet, I am physically fit and I have a regular sleep pattern	
In an organisational sense I am politically aware	
I realise an over-done strength can be a weakness	
My values and what is important to me underpin everything I do	
I have identified a clear style and personal brand for myself	
I am clear of my higher purpose in life	
I am a rounded whole person who is clear my job is only one role in my life	
I put into practice the actions needed to take me towards my visions	
I am interested in people and their success	
I have people around me that have different strengths to mine to underpin my weaknesses	
I look at the bigger picture	
I enjoy everything I do	
I am clear what my weaknesses are	
I am disciplined in my use of time towards my goals	
I use intuition to make decisions as well as logic	
I invest time in managing perceptions	
I lead my own life	

How do I rate on the success scale?

Scores

0–100

You are rating very highly on the failure scale and need to take action

101–200

Just starting out on your road to success – you have some serious work to do

201–300

You have made some progress in the success stakes but need to follow through what you know into action and perhaps learn a few new strategies

301–400

You are well on your way – keep going. Increase your success focus by 10% today and take action in the areas you have not scored highly.

401–500

You have nearly all the strategies in place to be a success – you are either there or just looking for the finishing touches

Section the First

Failure for Beginners – Mastering Yourself

Techniques that make sure you are mentally and physically prepared to go out and let the day take advantage of you.

Start as you mean to go on

It's a delightful day. It is filled with hopes and dreams that are just waiting to be seized. The sun is shining and the birds are singing in the trees – not the kind of birds that poo on you when you walk past, either. These are nice, polite, house-trained birds.

Of course, any minute now you're going to wake up. It's raining and you're not quite sure if the odd smell is coming from outside or from your insides. You spot your car parked under the tree outside. Have the birds treated it with suitable respect? Of course not – instead of deference they have chosen to defecate instead. The day has begun. Oh joy.

Now that you're feeling a little depressed you are in just the right state of mind to read on. This first failure lesson is an important one as it sets up the day nicely for maximum lack of achievement. We're talking about breakfast. People who regularly eat breakfast stay slimmer, are more mentally alert, and may even live longer than those who don't eat breakfast regularly.

People who eat a decent breakfast are better equipped to take on the office and win. Skipping breakfast, or any other meal for that matter, can lead to cravings and bingeing.

A study by the extremely clever folk at Harvard university and Massachusetts General Hospital found that students who usually ate breakfast had improved maths grades, reduced hyperactivity, decreased absence and tardy rates, and improved social interaction than students who rarely ate breakfast.

Moreover the pressures the subjects of this study were under were nothing compared to the cut and thrust of the workplace. So our initial advice to the student of failure would be to avoid breakfast as you would the waffle that fell behind the fridge a couple of weeks ago.

As weird as it sounds, skipping breakfast will probably make you fatter since you are more likely to snack on fatty and sugar-laden bits and bobs throughout the morning. This isn't good for your job prospects. A study by the UK's Personnel Today magazine found that 93% of human resource professionals would rather employ a 'normal' sized person over an obese one. It's great news for students of failure that so much can be achieved by just not eating.

Should you be forced into eating then let's have a look at just what will do you the most damage. A healthy breakfast would ideally include wholegrain cereal (bran flakes or fruit and fibre) and semi-skimmed milk or porridge. Wholegrain or wholemeal toast with olive oil spread is another option. These give you things like vitamin B for energy, protein to keep organs healthy and calcium to keep your bones nice and strong.

We're not nutritionists but apparently nuts and the like are also rather good. Combined with three lots of 20 minutes of exercise a week, two litres of water a day and five portions of fruit and veg a day and more likely than not you'll live for ever. (We've recently found out chips don't count as a vegetable portion by the way.)

> *"If you're not failing every now and again, it's a sign you're not doing anything very innovative."*
> Woody Allen – *director*

Of course all this stuff should to be avoided as far as we're concerned. Instead go for piles of sausages, fatty bacon and sugar-drenched muffins. Wash it all down with a nice glass of lard. If you need inspiration, look to such folk as the Mexicans, who drink more cola than milk every year.

SUCCESS WARNING!
Starting the day eating the right thing will prepare you mentally and physically for the day ahead. It will aid you in ways that you will probably never fully appreciate. Not eating properly will lead to a lack of concentration, irritability and weight gain in the long-term.

Always look on the dark side of life

If you focus on all your negative emotions and all the negative things that have happened to you in your life then you will be one miserable sod – just the kind of person we look for at the College. You can only begin to imagine how much fun the parties round here are.

There's nothing like wallowing in self-pity to leave you in as deep a rut as possible. If you stick at it, that rut will become so deep that not even the sturdiest of climbing gear will help you scale your way out.

They say every cloud has a silver lining. If you look back on things that at one time seemed momentous and insurmountable, you'll realise this is very seldom the case and by hook or by crook you got past the problem. It may be a cliché but it is reasonable to say that in most instances, nothing is as bad as it seems – unless of course you're paying any attention to these sagely pages.

If you do, your silver-lined clouds will slam together and produce thunder and lighting of truly biblical proportions. Keep it up and you'll soon have your very own weather front. It'll be like one of those cartoon clouds that follow morose characters around on TV and in magazines.

Your life will be like riding a bicycle with the brakes on. You will go on your journey but each peddle will be harder to turn than it ever needs to be. If you look at successful people, more often than not they don't seem to have a care in the world. Take it from us that this is not true. All the success literature calls on you to constantly feed yourself with positive messages. And this is what successful people do – they frame things in a more positive light and try to deal with issues rather than letting them fester.

It goes without saying then that a swamp of decayed and decomposing worries is exactly what you are after. If it all goes to plan then your storm front will keep the sludge in which you are standing nice and damp.

In Anthony De Mello's work 'The Heart of the Enlightened', he offers this suitably meteorological metaphor:

Traveller: What kind of weather are we going to have today?
Shepherd: The kind of weather I like.
Traveller: How do you know it will be the kind of weather you like?
Shepherd: Having found out, Sir, I cannot always get what I like, I have learned to always like what I get. So I am quite sure we will have the kind of weather I like.

The shepherd had accepted that when things didn't entirely go his way then he needed to adapt and get on with it. You, on the other hand, should be more like one of his sheep, who are probably very angry and hope the shepherd stops wittering on to passing strangers and gets on with a decent bit of shepherding.

Research by success expert Daryl O'Connor found there is a stronger correlation between resilience and success at the top of the organisation than there is IQ. He showed that if you keep bouncing back then you'll go far.

If you want to pinpoint what's going wrong then there's an easy exercise:

1. Recall your greatest failures in the following areas:
   - Your work
   - A major project
   - In a business relationship
   - As a leader
   - In your life
   - In a general non-business relationship
   - In a pastime, hobby or sport

2. Now identify the greatest lesson from each of the failures and write out how are you going to ensure you do not repeat the failure.

3. What patterns are you noticing?

4. What do you need to stop doing? Continue doing? Start doing?

5. What one thing if you did on a regular basis would have a positive impact on this area?

Either you can use this scheme to work out what went wrong and how you can alter it or you can use it to constantly remind yourself of how inadequate and generally useless you are. Of course we prefer the latter approach.

Make sure to repeat the mantra of self-defeat to yourself a few times each morning before you struggle out of bed to face a day that you know is not going to face you – it is going to run round and kick you on the behind.

SUCCESS WARNING!
If you look at successful people, more often than not they don't seem to have a care in the world. Not so – they think positively, are resilient and realise that the quickest way to get past things that are getting them down is to fix them. Constantly feed yourself with positive messages – look at past successes just to prove you've done it once and you'll do it again.

Being a shrinking violet

The good thing about top notch failure is that it doesn't have to be an overtly humiliating act for the failee. In fact some of the hardest, comprehensive and most conscientious work can lead to the most spectacular personal failures. Ancient philosophers called this 'the effort to recognition paradox' and it is based on the simple fact that you won't stick out unless you choose to.

Human beings just aren't that observant. Take the example of Daniela Simidchieva from Bulgaria. She is a mother of three with an IQ of almost 200 and has a mere five Masters degrees. Bulgaria's Mensa organisation has officially branded her the world's most intelligent woman. She is qualified as an English teacher, an industrial engineer and an electrical engineer but she can't get a job that pays any more than £90 a week. She claims that Bulgarian bosses just don't want clever staff.

If she's right then this makes Bulgaria a Mecca for students of failure and the country's economic outlook doesn't look good. As a truly successful student of failure you can work as hard as you like.

If you'd rather not duck, dodge and shirk (see later for more on this approach) feel free to put all your time into brilliant pieces of work. The key is to then never draw anyone's attention to all you've done and the successes you have had.

A potential danger point is when someone else tries to congratulate you – here everything hangs in the balance. Many unwary would-be failures have fallen into the trap of (albeit modestly) basking in their justified glory at this crucial time in the process. Instead, just blush and make those odd embarrassed gurgling noises that real failures make. These noises suggest you had help and would probably be liable for some kind of plagiarism if anyone actually dug deep enough into your work.

Yes, the background is the place for you – and the further back the better. You'll be pleasantly surprised at how little personal kudos you'll get if you get this right.

There are always examples of people who turned out to be very successful by taking these ideas to extremes. Take the example of Victorian soldier Garnet Joseph Wolsely, who was eventually made very famous in Gilbert and Sullivan's Pirates of Penzance as the 'Modern Major General'. His maxim was that if an officer wanted to do well he should try to get himself killed. Wolsely tried very hard to get himself done in. But in the end it got him noticed and he finished his days basically running the Army which was in turn running the globe under the British Empire.

The point for you is that you should hide, cower and generally become at one with the wallpaper. Hey presto: you've put in bucket loads of work and no one notices. It's really that easy. In fact, with any luck, your little sniffles will be the only thing that makes colleagues aware of your existence as yet another piece of dazzling labour is whisked away without so much as a by or leave.

Always sticking to being one of the crowd is a cornerstone of failure – so make sure you are never caught doing anything out of the ordinary. This is a noble calling – the people who have got this right are the unsung heroes of the office and of the College of Failure.

> "*The most important of my discoveries have been suggested by my failures.*"
> Humphrey Davy

And they will remain that way. There'd be statues built to their efforts if only anyone could remember quite what they looked like.

In conclusion: you have two choices. You can present yourself as a gazelle – filled with grace, speed and showing the promise of a sudden explosion of energy. Or you can be a cow – slow, lumbering and showing the promise of a sudden explosion of methane. Anyone for steak?

SUCCESS WARNING!
If you do great work, it is not enough. You need to gain visibility for it. Write a report, publish your results and accept the credit you deserve. Your boss and his boss will still need to know. On an ad hoc basis, do something out of the ordinary; be proactive, write a report or an article in the company newsletter. Build time into your schedule to gain visibility for your achievements.

Simply the best – better than all the rest

If the shrinking violet approach doesn't suit then there is another option open to you – this is to constantly bang on about how great you are. Tell your boss and everyone who will listen how brilliant your work is. If their ears start to bleed then you know you are getting it right.

The true connoisseur will not spend anytime on actually achieving anything, he or she will just brag all day. This will certainly make sure you are known; not in the way a successful person would want to be, but you will be known nonetheless. Remember the old adage: an empty vessel echoes the loudest.

Might we put the following example forward of an expert in this field who included this (absolutely true) covering letter when applying for an IT consultant role:

> I am a really clever man with an excellent brain and this is not my opinion (but I agree) this is the opinion of our customers. "Man with the Knowledge" this is the title from our customers. Sometimes they use higher epithets but I think this is mostly emotion.

Despite this unerring excellence this guy was looking for a job for some reason. We can't imagine why his previous employer would want to part with such an able fellow. If this is not example enough, let us impart the following tale that has been passed down from failure to son:

> *"Failure is, in a sense, the highway to success."*
>
> John Keats – *poet*

A turkey was chatting with a bull. "How I would love to be able to get to the top of that tree," sighed the turkey, "but I haven't got the energy." "Well, why don't you have a quick nibble on my droppings?" replied the kindly bull. "They're packed with nutrients." Despite some initial misgivings, the turkey had a nibble and found that he gained enough strength to reach the lowest level of the tree.

The next day he ate some more and soon found he could reach the second branch. On the fourth day of eating the bull's droppings the turkey finally found himself planted proudly on the top branch. The next day a passing farmer shot the turkey out of the tree. The morale of the story is: bullshit might get you to the top, but it won't keep you there.

SUCCESS WARNING!
Humility is very important – arrogance breeds dislike in others with consummate ease. Make the people who count aware of your success but never ram it down their throats. With a quiet, assured confidence be proud of your results.

Effort is too much like hard work

Successful people do what it takes to get the job done. So *you* need to focus on getting through the day with the least amount of work and hassle as possible. Concentrate on getting out as early as possible and make very sure you are never caught doing anything that might be construed as productive.

Who cares that the money you are given by your company allows you to run a car or perhaps buy a house? As a student of failure you just need to remember that work owes you a favour for being gracious enough to turn up.

In fact, any suggestion that you should go the extra mile for employers should be met with rank derision. This will excuse you from any of the arduous tasks which might lead to such unpleasant events as, say, promotion.

Might we suggest never giving more than 50% effort as a suitable benchmark? If you catch yourself doing more, take a well-earned moan – best directed at your colleagues we tend to find – and increase your stress levels by sitting around worrying about the things you could be doing.

You need to be 100% committed to being mediocre. Business guru, Jack Cranfield, says one should consider what would happen if you didn't give 100% and instead gave 99.9% every day. Applied to mundane daily activities he found:

- You would drink one litre of unsafe drinking water every month
- There would be two unsafe landings at Chicago's O'Hare International Airport each day
- 16,000 lost pieces of mail would be lost every hour
- There would be 20,000 incorrectly filled drug prescriptions every year
- 500 incorrect surgical operations would be performed each week
- 50 newborn babies would dropped at birth by doctors every day
- 22,000 cheques would be deducted from the wrong account each hour
- Your heart would fail to beat 32,000 times each year

There are two conclusions you could draw from this. First: putting in that extra bit of effort can make all the difference and will bring success and all its trappings. All it needs is the 0.1% and it will all add up. Second: you have power to create havoc to your career and the careers of others with the tiniest lack of effort. Here at the College we rather like that sneaking feeling of megalomania associated with the latter option!

> *"Our greatest glory is not in never failing, but in rising every time we fail."*
> Confucius – *philosopher*

SUCCESS WARNING!
Our results are equal to our endeavours and hard work. The cream does indeed always rise. It often doesn't take much extra effort to make things right or complete but it can make all the difference to your future successes. Remember employment is a bit like a relationship; it takes input from both sides to make it a success.

Money, money, money, it's not funny...

Work only for the money and be sure to tell everyone that is the only reason you pitch up day after day. If you put enough effort into this you'll begin to believe it yourself and this in turn will ensure you never enjoy your career.

They say money makes the world go round. One look in the newspapers makes clear just how unsuccessful a system this has turned out to be. Rather than spinning freely on an axis of cash, the world is about as stable as a drunk trying to walk in a straight line. Money does not make the world go round, happiness does. Money might be a part of that happiness but that's it.

Funnily enough, even those whose business it is to make money agree. Global investment bank Dresdner Kleinwort Wasserstein does deals worth billions of what ever currency you choose yet its economist James Montier said in his annual report that 'materialistic pursuits are not a path to sustainable happiness'. He concludes that money is 'a significant stumbling block on the path to happiness'. Instead he recommended taking more trips away and attending more concerts. It is not clear whether or not his employers decided he should go on a long trip himself after this...

With this reasoning in mind, we advise all students of failure to put all their effort into working for money alone, as it will inevitably mean a prolonged slog until the happy day that they pop their ill-fitting clogs.

Successful people tend to rise in the morning with a smile on their smug faces. You often find that these same scoundrels are in their second or third profession as they've dipped their toes in other arenas until they've found the one that fits. Mr Montier offers an explanation having analysed a series of psychological studies. This research concluded that people who chase the big bucks are more prone to delightful disorders such as paranoia, hysteria and attention deficit disorders among others.

On the other hand, when successful people pop their clogs it'll be more like the mouse in the windmill in Amsterdam, who sang every morning about how lucky he was and was way too upbeat for our liking. If you remember, the chorus went:

> *I saw a mouse!*
> *Where?*
> *There on the stair!*
> *Where on the stair?*
> *Right there!*
> *A little mouse with clogs on*
> *Well I declare!*
> *Going clip-clippety-clop on the stair*
> *Oh yeah*

> **"If you want to succeed, double your failure rate."**
> Thomas J Watson

We strongly advise you to avoid such Dutch, clog-related tomfoolery. Be happy with your miserable lot.

As a student of failure it is important to make sure you *really* dislike your work as there's a lot of competition in this field for award for top failure. Every year – normally about New Year unsurprisingly – about 40% of the population admit in various surveys that they can't stand their jobs and want to move. Of course they end up staying in their respective vocations for the money.

For this reason you will encounter folk on a daily basis who whinge, complain and carp on about the misery of their employment. The sheer volume of people who ascribe to this particular lesson means it's a dog-eat-dog scenario and something you have to really focus on if you want to out-tarnish the opposition. If you don't pay attention, they might show a greater disinterest than you and all sorts of successes could then come your way. It is remarkably easy to succeed if you just show a little enthusiasm so be really careful how you tread.

To make sure the boot of failure remains firmly on your sweaty foot, be the first to go off sick and when you return, even if you were genuinely sick, tell all your mates you went away for a long weekend. A truly dedicated student will keep an inventory of souvenirs in a cupboard at home; straw donkeys, kiss-me-quick hats and other such classy items – thus persuading your colleagues that you have been away on the Costas. Oh and don't forget the fake tan.

This behaviour could have the unexpected bonus of introducing you to some new associates who think you are *cool*. Look after these people like gold dust. Anyone who thinks such behaviour gives you credibility will be an invaluable ally in the battle for failure. Some folk call these people idiots; you must call them friends.

SUCCESS WARNING!

Our values are what drive, fuel and motivate us. Be clear what is important to you in the context of work and life in general – this is your mission and purpose in life. Write these values down and ensure that any role will satisfy them. This will mean work is not a burden but a seamless part of your whole life. It will allow you to jump out of bed in the morning looking forward to what the day will bring. Tell your boss and others what your values are, it will allow them to lead and motivate you in a way that will meet your needs.

Just say yes!

In today's warp speed world, things are getting faster and we are ever-more accessible through mobile phones, email, fax, phone, pager etc. As a student of failure you need to be sure that you keep an ear open for requests for your time and accept all the offers that are thrust your way. Successful people know when to say yes and when to say no to the numerous demands that are made of them. In short they know how to prioritise.

Everyone needs you. Your staff, boss, peers, suppliers, clients, the children's school, the six clubs each child belongs to, the gym where you work out, the child minder, the telesales people who cold call you each evening, your neighbours, extended family, friends, local charity dinners, your bank and mobile phone suppliers all come to mind after a cursory thought.

We have a full directory of others who will be happy to be a burden on your time at the College if you run out of ideas.

> *"The way I see it, if you want the rainbow, you gotta put up with some rain."*
> Dolly Parton

Nowadays there is just too much to do and so little time. This is great news for the student of failure and gives you the opportunity to always say 'yes' to every offer. Not only will you let people down left, right and centre, you will never be able to stick to your own priorities and life will become one big overbearing mess.

SUCCESS WARNING!

Be very clear about your life priorities and your work priorities. Take time to write down the four or five key foundations for each area. Then before saying yes to something stop and ask yourself: "Is this taking me towards one of my priorities or away from my priorities?" If it is not taking you towards your goals, be ruthless and discard the task.

In the zone

Always stay in your comfort zone and never take any risks. Then you can dream what might have been. Many an early student of failure has reported to us the weight of regret that lies on their elderly shoulders because they didn't seize an opportunity when it appeared before them. And the sole reason that they didn't seize said opportunity was because they found they were stepping out of their comfort zone.

These trailblazers sit for many an hour pondering the sheer volume of jealousy and bitterness that left a promising career in tatters. We are so proud of their dedication.

If you sit around and ignore opportunities when they arise it is logistically impossible to get ahead. Modern-day philosophers recommend that to be a success you should do one thing every day that scares you. The very idea of doing one thing every day that scares you, should itself scare you as far as we're concerned. It is the route to success.

Here's a fluffier way to illustrate the point.

A crow was sitting on a branch in a tree, doing nothing all day. He basked in the sun day-in and day-out as the world passed him by. Presently a small rabbit saw the crow and asked him: "Can I sit like you and do nothing all day long?" The crow looked lazily down and said: "Sure, why not?"

So the rabbit sat on the ground below the crow and joined his peaceful vigil. Suddenly a fox leapt out, jumped on the rabbit and ate it.

The moral of the story is: to be sitting doing nothing you need to be very high up indeed.

It's worth noting that if you do get up and start waddling about then things will still be fine if you make sure you don't set yourself any goals. Those tiresome folk that are forever moving on in the world and revelling in their success (they don't know what they're missing!) have a tiresome habit of having goals. This is not for you, trust us.

Successful people have goals.

Successful people have milestones so that however far away those goals might be there are always markers to show they are still on track. Successful people on this journey should just make you feel car sick.

Productivity and creativity guru Jurgen Wolff recommends milestones as they focus your mind on the benefits of your final outcome.

> *"I don't measure a man's success by how high he climbs, but how high he bounces when he hits bottom."*
>
> George S Patton –
> *military leader*

"The problem is that with long-term projects, the final results can be a long way off," he says. "So it's important to also establish milestones and find satisfaction in the process itself."

Milestones? Pah! Go for millstones instead; success markers that are forever out of reach and beyond your abilities in the short-term. This will make achievement seem like an impossible dream.

All in all, it's just safer to never set goals at all. That way you will never know how badly you are doing until it is too late. In fact you will be able to do things that are taking you in totally the wrong direction to where you want to go and you'll never even notice. Ignorance is indeed bliss! The only goal that can result from this is an own-goal. (Yes, we know how bad a joke that is, but it works.)

SUCCESS WARNING!

Take calculated risks – success is not about knowing it but doing it. You miss 100% of shots you do not take. If you take risks you might fail. If you don't take risks you will fail. Set yourself a vision of what you want to achieve. Then set goals and milestones along the way to allow you to measure and achieve success. Now, take action.

Fear factor

If you have a fear that stops you embarking on a journey towards success, be sure to forget the fact that psychologists believe that over 95% of fears have no real grounds at all. An oft used acronym for fear is: FALSE EVIDENCE APPEARING REAL.

It's true to say that the vast majority of worries have been made up by you (and the voices in your head) without any concrete evidence. (Rumour and hearsay do not count as evidence, by the way.) Take a moment to think of something that is hindering your progress – is there adequate evidence to say it's not just your own paranoia? If there is something, is it not easily overcome with a few words in the right ears?

If you take on board the idea that the vast majority of fears are without grounds then there's a likelihood you'll begin to have delusions of adequacy and this simply will not do in a student of failure. Freeze! Put down the self-assurance and go back into your comfort zone forthwith. Just who do you think you are? Overcoming fears is something for successful people.

A great example of this wings its way to us from Guayaquil – the biggest city in Ecuador. There Mayor Jaime Nebot hired a parrot to speak for him when he was asked 'undesirable questions' by the media which put him in awkward positions.

This fully paid up member of the venerable College of Failure brought out the parrot at a press conference and declared: "Here is a parrot that will be in charge to answer all the undesirable comments that I have no time to answer."

He tried to explain his folly, saying: "Some people only approach me with nonsense talk so the parrot will answer back in the same way because I need to use my time to work." These undesirable subjects included such trifling matters as social security policy.

The guy was too scared to try to take on the journos and just avoided the challenge. Now no one has any respect for him whatsoever.

When the voices start talking to you and letting you know that you are incompetent, inadequate and destined for failure it's quite easy to overcome them. Catch yourself making these negative statements and then repeat them to yourself in a ridiculously high pitched voice tone or in an absurdly exaggerated foreign accent. Think of the worries you normally feel before you go into conflict, are about to make a presentation or any other scary moment. Repeat this worry to yourself in your normal voice, then in Mickey Mouse's, then Donald Duck and then a sexy French voice. Now what was the difference? You can not take it seriously. Suddenly the worries aren't so worrisome any more.

It's worth remembering that all these worries are not really natural. When we are born we have only two fears – falling and loud noises. The rest we impose upon ourselves as we go along.

> *"If you have made mistakes, there is always another chance for you. You may make a fresh start at any moment you choose, for this thing we call 'failure' is not the falling down, but the staying down."*
>
> Mary Pickford – *actress*

SUCCESS WARNING!

You have the best coach in the world inside your own mind – the little voice that appears when you are talking to yourself. Natter away happily to yourself; give yourself positive reinforcement and encouragement. Lay down the gauntlet to your fears – take them on and more often than not you will win.

Best laid plans...

Forget planning, just sit back and wait for things to happen. Forget developing the skills you need – Lady Luck will take care of it. Successful people plan and manage their careers and the skills they need to get ahead. They ask themselves where they want to go and what they need to get there.

You should be less discerning as a student of failure. Take the example of convicted criminal Leandro Luis Sao Pedro who did a runner while on a day out from prison in Sao Paolo. He took our advice (we happened to be passing) and took the first opportunity that came along courtesy of our good friend Lady Luck.

In a truly immensely ill-planned move he got a job driving a prison bus. Shortly after he was arrested during a routine inspection. A local policeman told newspapers: "How dumb can you be? You escape prison and then get a job where you drive inside prison every week?"

> *"Failure is the opportunity to start again more intelligently."*
> Henry Ford –
> *car manufacturer*

If only the policeman could look behind the façade and appreciate Leandro's dedication to The Cause of Failure. Leandro – we salute you!

As far as planning for your future needs goes, it cannot be overstated how important it is that you avoid taking proactive steps to get training to improve your skills.

Not many people appreciate how many countries throughout the western world are suffering acute skills shortages. Improving your range of skills just a bit can mean a lot. In Britain alone there are about 640,000 unfilled vacancies because employers just can't get the people with the skills. One of those roles – perhaps a dream job – could be yours if you're not careful.

SUCCESS WARNING!

Be proactive: plan and manage your career. Constantly develop your skill set in line with your career vision. Ask yourself, do I have the skills I need for the level I am aiming for? Develop the skills NOW, so you have

them when you get there. As the technological age progresses high skills will be essential for success, whatever your profession.

Omniscience is a virtue

Go on, admit it – you know it all. There is nothing left for you to learn and no point of view that has merit unless it is your own. Successful people are always ready to listen and learn – they know that knowledge is power. You on the otherhand should just accept your own genius without question.

It has been said that the closest a person ever came to knowing everything that there was to know was Leonardo da Vinci. We at the School of Failure know this simply isn't the case. We know more and so do you – and what's more we will prove it in just a moment.

A motto for one to adopt might be:

'There was one occasion when I thought I'd got something wrong, but it turned out I was mistaken.'

If you accept this lesson and become a bona fide know-it-all, this presents a rather interesting dilemma – is there any point in proceeding with this course of failure? Why should you when you know it all already? Well perhaps we can offer you a new angle to your vast encyclopaedia of knowledge, so stick with it.

If people challenge you as to your omniscience there are two possible approaches (but of course you knew that.) One: a haughty look and a snort of derision should anyone think you are ripe for learning or other such enlightenment. This is followed by a short bout of ignoring said individual until they take their ignorance elsewhere. Two: simply prove you know more than Da Vinci because you've heard of him and it's very unlikely he knows who you are.

The dangers of those who wish to impose their 'knowledge' on you are everywhere. If you read a book, listen to an audio tape, speak to someone who is willing to share their experiences, or even attend a seminar or conference, never admit to yourself – or

The comedienne says...
"A man who smiles when things go wrong has thought of someone he can blame it on"

anyone else for that matter – that you did not know it all anyway. And don't contemplate anyone else's advice as this is a sure-fire way to learn – and consequently succeed.

Ensure your mind is closed – there is only one way to look at things and that is your way. Remember the key concept: if your brain is open, it's liable to fall out. That means someone's rug is going to get ruined, which is just plain rude.

SUCCESS WARNING!
Learn, learn, learn. Read books, heed the advice of others. Minds are like parachutes and only work when they are open. Take everything as an opportunity to learn. The right people always turn up so keep your radar focused and stay on the look out as you never know when or where this might be.

Laxtion man

Now that you are all-knowing it's time to take a breather. Time to rest on your laurels – you've earned it. Find the nearest comfy chair, choose the tipple of your choice and bask in the glory radiating from within you.

In this peaceful setting you might feel a certain uneasiness. Dear friend, without you realising it you may have come very close to disaster. You might have acted on your knowledge, whether it be real of imagined. This is why at the School of Failure we have formulated a cunning new errr…formula.

Instead of being a (wo)man of action – you should be a (wo)man of lax-tion. Yes, it is time to let any knowledge you might have go to wrack and ruin. Aim to have less energy than a sloth afflicted with M.E.

If you are desperate to attempt the folly of action then our tests have shown you'll probably get away with it if you make sure you only do it once. This at least allows you to reminisce over the aforesaid action which in turn allows you to tick it off the list of things that you've done and which are never to be done again.

But beware the sudden urge to try things a second time. Successful people know that the more times and the more things are attempted the greater the chance of success. If you look to actively put your expertise and passion to work then it's not a great leap of faith to realise you're likely to get results. Imagine if one morning a young Alexander the Great had rolled over in bed and thought: "I can't be bothered with conquering the world, it's just too much like hard work." There are two certain consequences: One – we'd not have a critically-panned blockbuster about it starring Colin Farrell with some utterly absurd highlights. Two – he'd have to be known as Alexander the Mediocre or perhaps just Alex.

The spur to get up and do something is a trap into which many unwary students of failure have fallen. This is why all dictionaries in the College have had the pages with the word 'proactive' on them removed.

Now sit back again in your comfy chair as before sip your beverage and wait for the moment of unease to pass. That was a close run thing.

SUCCESS WARNING!

Put your knowledge and skills to good use – seize opportunities as they arise. Constantly seek improvement. Displaying flexibility and adapting to circumstances as they arise is key. As the Romans used to say: carpe diem – seize the day.

> *"Learn from the mistakes of others. You can't live long enough to make them all yourself."*
> Eleanor Roosevelt – US 1st lady

Hat-trick

We have talked about how successful people set goals for themselves and how as a student of failure it is important you ignore this idea altogether. However, we are quite happy for you to set targets for yourself, as long as they are totally immeasurable and unrealistic. We have referred to these unattainable goals as 'millstones' rather than 'milestones'. Now let's take a closer look at just what differentiates one from the other…

Trainers (people who train, not shoes) the world over have used the acronym SMART to inspire people to success. We will only tell you what this means if you promise to ignore it. It stands for Specific, Measurable, Action-based, Realistic, Timed. These are the chief tenets of successful goals and the milestones that guide you there.

Let us ignore this wisdom one step at a time. If you have been foolish enough to set yourself goals and mini goals (milestones) along the way, make sure they are wasted by failing to put a deadline date on any of them – that way you can bumble on without making progress and not care. You have made your progress immeasurable in one easy swoop.

Having done this, it's time to make your milestones unrealistic. A successful person will stretch themselves, but they will make the goal ultimately achievable. They will push and push themselves but they get there in the end. Your goals need to be so unrealistic the only sensation of pushing that you experience is that of trying to shove water uphill. There is nothing more depressing than goals that just can't be achieved. These are true millstones of failure around your neck and they will drag you down. Isn't that a thought to lift your heart?!

The case of a UK leadership organisation that recently decided it was going to find 'the World's Most Outstanding People' springs to mind. We followed this quest for a while until we realised that it was a thoroughly futile effort and began to lose interest. Of course, before we parted ways we made sure to encourage them never lower the bar on this adventure. To our knowledge, years later, they're still at it, if they haven't been eaten by cannibals while canvassing for applicants in darkest Africa. Dr Failingstone, I presume?

When a milestone is missed you need to look on this failure as the end of the world. That's it, it's all over. Saonara, caio, tchuss, au revoir, chocks away. This is the creed of the true failure.

Successful people take a moment to look back at and celebrate all the successes that have got them to this point. They realise that missing one milestone is just a blip. They will look at why things went wrong and how they might be done better. Some will even have several projects going at once so that they can move onto another to recharge their batteries. You'd be amazed what a short time away from a problem can do to put it in perspective.

For this reason we are very single-minded at the College.

Finally, should you be forced into setting some kind of realistic goal, all is not lost. Manoeuvre yourself into a position so that there will be absolutely no benefit to you. Aim to help everyone else but you – this will reduce your motivation totally.

> *"Failure is the condiment that gives success its flavour"*
>
> Truman Capote – *author*

SUCCESS WARNING!

The goals you set need to be meaningful to you – you need to have an emotional attachment to them and they need to inspire you. They need to be smart and achievable, yet also stretching, so you go further than even you believed you could. Ask yourself: what is in it for me? What are the benefits? What will you gain? And what will you lose if you do get it? What pain will you feel? When you have set the goals, write them down and tell other significant people who have an interest what your goals are. Each person you tell will increase your commitment.

Low Fidelity

There's nothing more sickening than the chap who will turn to you while you are revelling in your failure and blurt out: "Have faith – it'll be o.k!" Not only is this annoying, it is usually true.

People who believe in themselves go far. Successful folk throughout history have shown that they believe in themselves absolutely and if things go wrong they will bounce back. Take these two quotes; they were said thousands of years apart yet they have an eerily similar message:

> "Our greatest glory is not in never failing, but in rising every time we fail."
>
> Confucius

> "If you want to succeed, double your failure rate."
>
> Thomas J Watson, founder of IBM

Self-belief is a dangerous commodity for the student of failure. These questing folk, such as Mr Watson, tend to look at the bigger picture and not let the little things get them down. It's remarkably easy to believe you are a failure as long as you tell yourself you are one on a regular basis and at all times look out for evidence that proves you are.

Much of the evidence you seize upon will be insubstantial in the scheme of things but there's no need to remember that. Remember the stats we gave you about 95% of fears either being in your head or being of no consequence? Well forget them now. Instead grab a trowel and like some kind of Godzilla-esque garden pest, make mountains out of all your mole hills.

Successful people appreciate that examples of failure are something to be learned from and overcome. These sorts of people just don't have the kind of earth-moving equipment you have – their mole hills will remain just that.

While the successful folk look onwards and upwards, you, dear student, should (for once) refuse to accept the easy way out. Instead be incredibly hard on yourself. If you achieve eight out of ten targets, make sure to focus on the bits you did not fulfil.

Beat yourself up over these at every opportunity. This beating can be on a metaphoric or physical level, dependent on how the mood takes you. (However, do make sure you soak anything that gets blood on it in cold salty water ASAP. A free tip from our mothers there.)

Always focus on how far you have got to go rather than how far you have come and what you have achieved. There's nothing more depressing than counting up all the things you have yet to do and ignoring the things that have gone so well – this is why we are all for it!

If you're going to put in this kind of effort, do make sure you share your self-loathing with your colleagues. The British culture was built on the irrevocable stiffness of our upper lips. No matter how people think we've moved from

> **"Nothing fails like success because we don't learn from it. We learn only from failure"**
> Kenneth Boulding –
> *thinker*

the Victorian days, this virtue is still prized above almost any other. People will be sympathetic to the plight of one who seems down and might be even offer to help but they will not abide people who wallow in self-pity. It's just not on, don't you see?

So get that top lip wobbling like jelly! This is a sure fire route to alienation among your colleagues who will avoid you and your immediate surroundings which will come to resemble a black hole sucking the energy out of the office.

For successful people there's a really good way to focus on the task at hand if they find that they are scared and can't concentrate. This technique comes from the world of sport where they say that "fire is in the heart but ice is in the head". This is why the teams line up for the anthems and stare so fiercely forward while the camera goes by. In the old days they would get very angry and hop about, head-butting walls and the like to prepare themselves. Now they focus all that energy on success and don't waste it being nigh-on deranged. This is how it works...

Often when you are very nervous, you become really hot and your heart races and feels like it is ready to leave your body notwithstanding your ribcage being in the way. To calm it, fix your stare at a single spot and while staring at the spot become gradually aware of what is happening on either side of it. Slowly extend your peripheral vision to take in your surroundings and you will find that your pulse slows, you gain a more relaxed perspective about what you are about to do, and your heart stops – not completely obviously – but the heavy pounding will be gone. In short – you calm down.

How does that work?

It comes from the fight and flight response when our ancestors were hunting or being hunted by animals with very big pointy teeth. When hunting they needed a narrow, focused vision to fix on the animal and enable them to get their prey. Similarly when running away they needed to fix on a landmark in the distance to ensure that they took the straightest and fastest route to get away. When they were relaxed and resting, their vision needed to be wide, enabling them to see what was happening around them. It's basically the same today, although instead of big pointy teeth coming after you, it's more likely to be the forked tongue of your boss or bank manager.

> *"If you try to fail and succeed, which have you done?"*
> George Carlin – actor and comedian

SUCCESS WARNING!
People who believe in themselves tend to go far as history repeatedly demonstrates. Just keep reminding yourself you can do it and look back to your previous successes – they are not one-offs, they are a mark of your innate ability. Only one person can take away your self-belief – and that is you.

Value added failure

We've talked about having goals and the importance of avoiding these dangerous signposts to success. Next write down all your values ask yourself what is important to you in the context of work. You should aim to have a list of seven or eight values.

There is no doubt that someone on the long and straight road to success should know what's important to them and this is why coaches the world over tell their charges to write down these seven or eight values. We'd encourage you to do this too, but only so you know just what you need to avoid.

Now take these values and put them in order – one being the most important down to eight being the eighth most important. Then ask yourself: are these currently being met in your role? Put a percentage of total satisfaction that you feel at this point for each value. The higher the percentage the greater chance of success.

Setting personal values allows successful people to tailor their progress to their own needs and allows them to make as rapid progress as possible. But very few people choose to live by their own values – they adopt those of others. This is like putting on a random suit and hoping it will fit. The chances are it will not fit; it will either hang off you and smother you or it will constrict the life out of you.

Successful people do not automatically do as they are told – they look inside themselves and ask what is important to them; not what other people expect them to consider important.

Adopting another person's values is the easy way out and for this reason we at the College are all for it. Do what ever your father or mother did for a living. The fact you hate numbers and can not add up is irrelevant – become an accountant like your father. If this doesn't suit you, then perhaps your boss's recommendation that you'll go far in envelope stuffing will do the job.

Do what everyone else tells you you should but what ever you do don't take time out to consider if it is really for you and whether it plays to your strengths and makes you happy. That way lies success, compadre.

SUCCESS WARNING!
Our values fuel us to achieve in what we do and enjoy life. Don't ever accept the values that are thrust upon you by those close to you or society at large without questioning whether they fit with what drives you.

Mirror, mirror on the wall, who's biggest failure of them all?

Take a moment to look at yourself in the mirror. Is the figure looking back at you in control of its destiny? Is it confident of success and its trappings? Are the shoulders straight back and the bearing noble? If they are then it's important you read on with care. Successful people carry themselves in a manner that shows they are a success. From the moment you walk into a room you can get a good idea of who is on the up just from their baring.

Try this little exercise that actors do before they go on stage for a performance:

- Reach up as high as you can
- With your arms in the air, let your wrists go floppy, then your elbows, then your shoulders so that your arms fail by your side

- Letting your arms dangle limply and with your knees slightly bent flop down so your arms are dangling towards the ground

- Try and relax every muscle in your body

- Now imagine the vertebrae in your spine are building blocks

- Roll back upwards picturing your vertebrae stacking up on top of one another

- When your back is straight keep going as if a string were pulling you from the top of your head and you feel a bit like you are looking over an imaginary wall.

- You might find your shoulders are up round your ears. Let them relax

- Congratulations, you now have good posture.

> *"Success isn't built on success. It is built on failure and frustration, sometimes catastrophe, and learning to turn it around"*
> Sumner Redstone – media mogul

Now we have established how a successful baring looks, we need to make sure you avoid this and so we have created a failure exercise programme. Don your leotard or lycra and join in... Let the shoulders slump, 2, 3, 4 and slump, 2, 3, 4. Now eyes focusing on the feet, 2, 3, 4, feet, 2, 3, 4. Bend the back slightly and 2 and 3 and 4. The way you carry yourself will automatically impact on the way you feel. Look at meerkats in the desert – can you picture them being alert and ready for danger while kicking back in a little mongoose armchair? Thought not.

So put this little failure exercise into practise and you'll find yourself physically prepared for the brow beating that is coming your way.

If there's no room to be flinging your arms about as in the actors technique above then there's a more subtle approach which is an excellent way to relieve tension and is known as the DBC – the Double Bum Clench. (Bet you didn't see that coming!)

Have you heard the term 'being centred'? The most vulnerable part of our body is the stomach and this is the same with all animals. Think of wild horses: where do the dogs, lions or other such predators attack them? It's in the stomach because the rest of the body has bone to protect it. This centre of tension also stems from the old fight or fight syndrome where you tense up before a demanding occasion; your adrenalin pumps, your centre rises and you get the dry throat and the butterflies start careering round like there's some kind of World War I dogfight going on in your stomach.

So, onto the DBC... If you want to calm yourself and break the build up of tension, the technique is simple; you tense or squeeze your backside muscles, relax them, and then relax again. All at once you will feel your centre drop and you will feel centred and calmer. There you have it, The Double Bum clench.

The art of failure requires that others blame you, control you, and do all they can to make you feel insecure. So as you'll appreciate, the right demeanour is an important start, which is why we offer the techniques of good posture and the DBC as examples of things to avoid. (Although you can probably put people right off their dinner if you make too obvious use of the DBC.)

Now let's look at your state of mind. If you have bought this book, there's every chance that you are somewhere in a civilised world of laws, regulations and probably book shops. (Or coffee tables. If this is the case then go and buy your own copy, you cheapskate.) This offers you opportunities and freedoms that the vast majority of human beings will never have the luxury of even contemplating.

> *"If there exists no possibility of failure, then victory is meaningless"*
>
> Robert H Schuller –
> *author*

Despite this, a lot of people believe that they are trapped by a society that has chosen a place for them and will not allow them to go anywhere else. These people are your fellow students of failure.

Unless you are some kind of crazed conspiracy theorist, who thinks the government is out to get him or her and who sleeps with a variety of weapons close to hand, it's actually quite easy to appreciate that things are actually weighted in your favour.

Take the example of the world cut down to only 100 people. If you did this you'd see just how lucky you are. In a world of 100 people, using present global ratios, 80 would live in substandard housing. 70 would be unable to read. Only one would have a college level education and only one would own a computer. 75 people would not have food in the fridge. Many of these 75 would not have the means to go out and get it either.

It is estimated that three billion people live in a society where you cannot speak your mind or practise your religion without fear of persecution.

Does this put your so-called 'depressing' existence in perspective? Successful people tend to notice and seize this opportunity.

As a dedicated student of failure, you need not bother yourself with such trivia. Even though you control how you think and feel – and probably do so without fear of persecution – allow yourself to feel insecure. Worry and then worry some more. Make a habit of being concerned about everything and forget that you're probably one of the luckiest people on God's green earth.

Look at the late lamented and utterly mental Howard Hughes for inspiration. Having created a vast empire based upon innovation in the field of commercial aviation, he ended up living in a paper suit in the desert somewhere in Nevada. Why? He started to worry about everything; right down to the germs that he insisted were all around waiting to strike.

So never mind that you are privileged beyond belief compared to most other human beings. Keep worrying about how the world is against you. If you worry enough we'll throw in the hidden bonus of a stomach ulcer – never let it be said we aren't generous folk here at the College of Failure!

SUCCESS WARNING!

Successful people switch off the auto-pilot of negative emotions, fear and worry. They consciously decide on how they want to think and feel. They realise just how lucky they are and that most worries are mere trifles. This is why you will see them standing up straight. They will not be bowed.

Do worry, don't be happy

To aid the process of self-vilification there is one simple step you can take: don't ever smile. Look at the physics of it: you use an average of 43 muscles for a frown. You use an average of 17 muscles for a smile. Every two thousand frowns create one wrinkle. The great news is you will not only moan a lot, you will look old quicker, die younger and be less likely to achieve anything – Utopia as far as we are concerned.

There is lots of research that shows that smiling laughing and being happy can increase your life expectancy and releases endorphins in the body to make you feel really good. It lifts people around you and makes you more attractive. Of course we don't approve of this kind of nonsense, so knit those eyebrows ASAP.

Happiness can throw a spanner in the failure works from the very beginning of a career, so avoid it at all costs. Studies have found that a person who can make a recruiter laugh is more likely to get a job. If you can then make your employers laugh over time you tend to earn more in bonuses. The reason is simple – a person of good humour engages others more successfully – even if it is only by making them smile.

> *"What is defeat? Nothing but education. Nothing but the first step to something better"*
>
> Wendell Phillips –
> *American abolitionist*

If you must insist on trying to be funny, then we recommend you go for liberal amounts of sarcasm as the study found that this negative form of humour could offend just as easily as it could amuse.

The successful person will be a pleasure to be around and still be credible. As always you can take things way too far and just become annoying. Separate research found that the 'office joker' even out-paced the 'white van man' as the most annoying person people come into contact with in the working environment. So slip on that garish suit and kiss-me-quick hat and get to work.

SUCCESS WARNING!

If you think about it, everything you list as things that you want to achieve to be a success are things that would make you happy. Happiness and success go hand in hand. Even if you have to start small – with a smile – having a happy outlook on life will help immeasurably.

Knowledge is sour

While this book is justifiably recognised by many as the leading journal in its field, we recognise that it is important to draw on the works of those that came before for inspiration.

So in a move that will positively disgust our publisher, let's have a brief look at the best selling personal development book by another of our colleagues – the 7 *Habits of Highly Effective People* by Stephen Covey.

> *"Just because something does not do what you planned does not mean it's useless"*
> Thomas S Edison – *inventor*

As you'll appreciate you are on dangerous ground here since folk like Covey have taught success with...err...success for years. We offer his wisdom just so you know your enemy and thus know what to avoid.

Covey is a great failure model if you choose to ignore his guidance at just the right moments. He gave the world the Circle of Concern. This encapsulates the things that are an outstanding drain on our energy.

Using pen and paper, draw a circle with every problem, issue or concern you currently have listed inside it. Once you have done this read through them each day. Successful folk will work out ways round these concerns or will realise they probably aren't as serious they first thought. They can then be removed from the circle and either put to one side or left behind. For you they are merely a reference point to remind you just how miserable things are; a constant reminder of your pain and suffering and how everything is just *so unfair*.

So draw your circle and list your concerns. Use crayons if you see fit – anything that will bore your inadequacies into your skull on a daily basis. If you have access to any neon lighting, then all the better.

You will soon find yourself rendered immobile by your concerns and unable to do anything about it. Are you feeling paralysed yet? Well done! It's time to move on.

SUCCESS WARNING!

Successful folk realise that the mere act of writing their concerns down will put things into perspective. This in turn will make them realise they probably aren't as serious they first thought. They will then transfer their concerns into their circle of influence and actually control the situation by doing something about them. If you are concerned about X, Y and/or Z then do something about it now.

Honesty is the worst policy

We have seen how absurd it is to tell the truth to colleagues and friends if you wish to reach true Zen-failure. We turn now to lying on a slightly more philosophical level – the fine art of self-denial.

Lying in its basic state does not require you to actually believe your own lie. The wisdom of the past masters – black belts in the Art of Failure – has shown that to master the self is truly to master failure. You have to convince yourself of your own inadequacy. If you wish to light some candles now and adopt the lotus position, then please go ahead.

It is time to get to know your inner failure.

The essential lesson here is to never be honest with yourself. We have already stressed the need to concentrate on your failures and ignore your successes. Successful people tend to be optimistic in the face of adversity; they take heart from their achievements as they provide the fuel to keep them going. Students of failure deny themselves this luxury and wallow in self-pity. Self-loathing is a delightful addition to your failure armoury.

But even greater failure can come from looking at the other end of the spectrum. This is all about kidding yourself that you are brilliant at everything – even if the evidence is there that you have been less than successful.

Turn a blind eye to your genuine inadequacies and continue with what you are doing and how you are doing it. If you do this there's no way you can improve.

This might sound absurd to any right-minded person. Yet look about you and clock all the colleagues you have who make mistake after mistake and never seem to learn from it. These individuals are your fellows at the College of Failure. If we had a special handshake we'd recommend you go and do it now. However, we don't, so we won't.

It takes very little to differentiate you from these folk. Taking a look at how a project has gone and noting where you could have done things better will immediately mark you out from the failures around you. If you then act upon these notes you're well on the road to success nirvana. But that's for the successful types. It goes without saying then that blissful ignorance is your path.

"Failure is good. It's fertilizer. Everything I've learned about coaching, I've learned from making mistakes"
Rick Pitino – *basketball coach*

The more senior you are the more damage you can reap with your wilful self-delusion. Take al-Saadi Gadaffi, son of the Libyan dictator, Colonel Gadaffi. Young Gadaffi was captain and striker of Tripoli football club Al-Ittihad who won several medals and tournaments. This doesn't sound like the success story we should be modelling ourselves on does it? But if you delve a little deeper you find the ideal failure case study.

You see al-Ittihad wasn't actually doing too well. Gadaffi was head of the Libyan Football Association and made a habit of ignoring his team's lack of success and just showered them with medals and trophies whether they played any games or not. He also sacked the

Libyan international coach who dropped him from the national team, despite the team having some notable successes after he was left on the bench.

His dad, Colonel Gadaffi was no better when he said: "The Libyan army is capable of destroying America and breaking its nose." This kind of family-sized self-denial is exactly what we're after.

SUCCESS WARNING!

Self-awareness is fundamental to building emotional intelligence and being clear on your strengths, weaknesses and defence mechanisms. Successful people are always honest and realistic with themselves. This way you can analyse why things went wrong, learn from your mistakes and move on. This doesn't mean making everyone aware of your inadequacies or failures. You should only do this if it is going to impact on other members of a team or if it means someone will be able to give you constructive advice on where you went wrong.

Beg, borrow and steal, steal, steal

Nicking bits and bobs from work is something that has been going on ever since the first caveman took home his office cave painting brushes to decorate the extension he had just chiselled into his semi-detached cave. And why not? He had to keep up with the Uggh family next door, after all.

This ethos is one that has existed for millennia and one that the student of failure should embrace.

Ignore the fact your company pays you money to do a job and ensure you fiddle your expenses at every opportunity.

"Men succeed when they realise that their failures are the preparations for their victories"

Ralph Waldo Emerson –
poet

You could make an extra £3.50 on that trip to Manchester. Take home computer discs, pens, paper, sticky tape, staplers and all the stationery you can fit into your bag. Remember that the stationery cupboard is for two things only:

1. Kitting out your house with all the writing materials you will ever need.
2. Misbehaving in after the Christmas party.

This is a lifestyle choice you are making. If you can convince yourself that relocating large amounts of office property to the safety of your own home is an o.k thing to do, then you're starting a vicious circle. The company then has to spend more replacing your ill-gotten gains which in turn means less money for investment, which in turn means less money and opportunity for you.

Moreover, no one likes a thief. Even if it is something really insignificant you nick, the fact is you are still happy to break the eighth Commandment and if you are willing to do that, then there's every reason others will suspect you'd be willing to do them a mischief too. Stick with it and you'll soon be breaking other commandments such as coveting the boss's partner.

Highlight your thieving ways by bragging about it – it's worth taking pride in what you do after all. If you don't know where to start you could highlight your misdemeanours using the following joke, which we are prepared to admit is awful:

A thief broke into the local police station and stole all the lavatory equipment. A spokesperson was quoted as saying, "We have absolutely nothing to go on."

One last message that may chill you, dear student, but stick with your pilfering and dishonesty for all our sakes as it will pay off in the failure stakes. That message is from the ancient philosopher Horace, who said:

Raro antecedentem scelestum deseruit pede poena claudo.

Of course we don't need to tell you this means 'Justice, though moving slowly seldom fails to overhaul the fleeing villain'. They say if you live by the sword, you die by the sword. They also say the pen is mightier than the sword. Imagine then the danger you're getting into if you live by the stolen pen...

> **"Problems are to the mind what exercise are to the muscles, they toughen and make strong"**
> Norman Vincent Peale – *self-help guru*

SUCCESS WARNING!

Successful people value honesty, trust and transparency in the way they communicate and the way they run their lives. They set high standards in what ever they do and they stick to them. Others will recognise and value you in turn.

Handling rejection

Rejection is a natural part of life. Fortunately, very few people can accept this and so we get a steady stream of insecure and down-heartened folk coming through the ornate doors of the College. Once enough have come through, we'll have our personal cult and we'll be able to build the moat and portcullis we've been after for so long in order to keep our acolytes within the walls.

And don't doubt our two-up, two-down semi-detached castle will be a reality soon because it takes a strong person to accept that rejection is nothing more than a state of mind.

Successful people throughout the ages have been marked out by their ability to accept rejection and try again. Take the following:

- It took wannabe crime novelist, John Creasey, 743 straight rejection slips from publishers before someone was wise enough to take his manuscript. Over sixty million of his books have now been published.
- How about Thomas Edison who took a good thousand attempts before getting the electric light bulb right? When someone asked him: "How did you keep going after you had failed more than a thousand times?" Edison replied, "I did not fail a thousand times; I learned a thousand ways that didn't work."
- The first words that Sir Edmund Hillary, the famous mountaineer and conqueror of Everest, heard from his school gym instructor were: "What will they send me next?"
- "Balding, skinny, can dance a little." A casting director on Fred Astaire at his first audition.
- Beethoven's music teacher concluded that the creator of some of

the greatest classical masterpieces of all time was "hopeless" at composing.

If this happens to you, don't pick yourself up and dust yourself off. Instead find a hole to jump into so you can get even lower than you ever thought possible. If you take a shovel with you to keep digging then the possibilities are endless. Students of failure are entitled to a free shovel if you pop round for a visit. Don't believe it when they tell you Cook discovered Australia; when he got there he was greeted by our students who had taken this digging metaphor to extremes and tunnelled their way there a few years previously.

> *"Failure is a detour, not a dead end street"*
>
> Zig Ziglar –
> *motivational speaker*

It's actually quite easy to get the whole 'picking up and dusting off' process going. You see all our memories are on chains and are linked by emotion. Think of a time in your life when you were feeling really positive, had a sense of achievement, felt relaxed or were with people you totally trusted.

Recapture the good feelings, the happiness, the positive thoughts you felt about yourself and your ability to achieve at that time. Imagine you are there right now, seeing what you saw, hearing what you heard and feeling what you felt inside. You will then feel that way again.

Of course this is the way of the successful person and rejection for you should be a nail in your own custom-made coffin. For the students of failure rejection is to be regarded as a personal attack on who you are and what you stand for, despite the fact it will almost inevitably not be.

When faced with denial and dismissal some people fight back (this is how folk built whole nation states in the early days), others become slaves to failure.

SUCCESS WARNING!

Successful people do not see failure as failure or as a rejection. They see it as an opportunity to learn and take a step nearer to success. Failure is not falling down, it is staying down.

A measure of success

As anyone who has ever followed sport will know, keeping a tally of results is key to any team. While it allows you to remember just which member of the team deserves your self-righteous sofa-based wrath for his or her bad performance, in the hands of the unwary it can also act as a very good motivational tool.

People are fuelled by keeping lists, scores and results to measure their achievement. It reminds you in your darkest hour of the successes you have had and will strike a chord that allows you to pick yourself up. Successful people realise that every little bit helps and so they keep these lists – whether they be physically written down or just a few nice mental reminders – because they can and do make a difference.

Here's an odd aside for you while we're on the matter of lists: why do psychiatrists always seem to have the most plaques on their walls? Is it because they need to constantly be reminded of their competence because they themselves are shockingly insecure? Should it be you on the couch or should it be them? Who is the real patient? If that's not enough to fry your brain then we give up.

So keep a daily list of anything you have failed at, lost at or have performed in a mediocre manner. It will be a constant reminder of the failure that you have so lovingly embraced.

SUCCESS WARNING!

Successful people not only have goals and targets – they also keep track of scores and results and therefore measure their achievements. This gives them a memento of their abilities that they can keep with them even in their darkest hours.

Keeping a wobbly upper lip

The British have always been good at the stiff upper lip. It served us well until people realised we couldn't bluster our way round the globe forever subjugating other nations with the merest flick of our enormous moustaches.

> *"You don't drown by falling in water, you drown by staying there"*
> Edwin Louis Cole – *author*

It was long held that the concrete which bound our success together lay within that stiffest of upper lips. In the olden days our explorers probably could have cut through diamonds with theirs given half a chance.

But things change. Without becoming an utter wet lettuce (something guaranteed to get on people's wick even in this day and age), research has shown that getting in touch with your emotions can be really helpful to you (well not *you*, but those seeking success).

The brain is programmed to remember events that have strong emotions attached and as such your memory can be improved if open yourself to them. A study published in the Journal of Research and Personality (there is a journal for absolutely anything by the way, if you take the time to look), found that subjects who actively tried to hide their emotional responses couldn't remember things so well.

Boffins at Stanford University and the University of Austin, Texas asked a set of people to subdue their emotions as much as possible while watching a film. When compared with another group who were letting it all hang out, they found the first group couldn't remember the film nearly so well.

Either this is good news for the students of failure as it gives scientific grounds to our ranting or it's just because the first group thought the film was rubbish.

Showing emotions also gives you a human side that others can relate to – you will always go further if you can interact with people. That said, our students of failure are asked to put up defences, (wo)man the walls, and prepare to repel borders if someone tries to provoke an emotional reaction from them. They say no man is an island. That's not to say a man can't be a fortress of emotional detachment with a moat so big that island status must surely beckon sooner or later.

Lastly, if you bottle things up all the time - especially when things seem to be going wrong, sooner or later you will explode. It takes courage to confront difficult situations. If you dwell on things that annoy you, paranoia will grow and soon you'll be howling at the moon. Then the emotional explosion will come – this may be literally or it may be figuratively – either way it's not going to be pretty for anyone.

SUCCESS WARNING!
Embrace your emotions, don't bury them. They are an aid to memory and they allow you to interact with colleagues and friends more effectively. It also means unpleasant situations tend to get resolved quicker and are not allowed to fester and grow bigger than they ever needed to be.

Relationships – failure has a partner

Relationships in business and life are fundamental for success. Relationships are the container everything else fits into. We have therefore devoted the following six sections to this subject to give you the maximum opportunity to mess up this vital area.

It is not just your imagination, it is harder to find and keep a good long-term relationship than it was some years ago. Dwell on that depressing thought for a moment. Good, let's move on.

Often when we see people who have a good relationship we are tempted to say "aren't they lucky!" Well luck has little to do with it. It's a mixture of hard work, good communication and some compromises – all facets that are strictly forbidden at the College of Failure, you'll be pleased to hear. Anyway you're basically married to the College now anyway – it's a lifelong commitment you know, this failure lark.

Research has shown that the secret to successful relationships comes down the following six areas:

1. Communication
2. Commitment and trust
3. Freedom

4   Friendship and Support
5   Working at your relationship
6   Learn to love yourself

With this outline in mind we can look at just how you can contrive to scupper any chances with that promising stationery cupboard romance you are having with Wendy and/or Dave from accounts.

The fundamentals to good business relations are the same as good personal relations so apply the following lessons as you will.

1   Communicating

Talking openly and honestly is the number one way to make a relationship successful.

> *"The only failure one should fear is not hugging to the purpose they see as best"*
>
> George Eliot – author

Listening and showing you are interested as well as revealing secrets and personal information while knowing you are not going to be judged are the ingredients to successful communication.

If you were to visit the College of Failure, you would find a set up that closely resembles a 14th century nunnery. Aside from our strange choice of dress (an odd 'habit' one might say), this cloistered existence means we get little chance to talk to one another and frequent misunderstandings ensue.

Our arguments tend to spring from who ate the last bit of cheese, but feel free to tailor this to your own needs.

Four steps you will want to avoid as they tend to encourage open and honest conversations:

- Let the other person know that talking about issues is important to you
- Be open yourself and share things that are important to you
- Ask questions
- Don't assume if the other person is silent that it means disinterest.

People talk for the fun of it, to solve problems and to ask for what they want. (At the College we encourage just talking for the sake of imposing yourself on others – they hate it.) If you take a moment to listen to what another person is saying and engaging with them it will make a connection between the two of you. If you listen to feelings you will have an instant guide to what response to make. There are four basic feelings and how the successful folk will expect you to react:

- Angry – give the person space and take them seriously
- Sad – lots of support and consideration
- Scared – talk through their fears and make some plans to change the situation
- Happy – laugh, dance, sing or whatever you do to celebrate!

We think these reactions are fine as long as you mismatch them in the most imaginative manner you can. So, for example, if you meet an angry person, laugh and dance. Then duck.

2 Commitment and trust

Many people are afraid of commitment. The truth is that commitment happens in small stages. Commitment starts with trust.

The first time we meet people we acknowledge them and we make many assumptions about them that might be right or they might be wrong. Unconsciously we ask ourselves: "is this person like me, because if they are like me then I like them". This means you can manipulate people without them even knowing it.

The technique is called 'mirror and match'. If you sit in a similar manner and copy the mannerisms of your target they will unconsciously warm to you. Put in mathematical terms one might say *similarity = influence and rapport*. However, don't copy people exactly or they will think you're some kind of freak or kidnapper. This is illustrated by the true story of a junior manager who found himself in a pub alone with his CEO. He had been on a course which had covered the mirror and match technique but was a little too keen and copied the boss exactly.

Suddenly the CEO jumped up and started waiving his arms around. He turned to his underling and asked: "Aren't you going to copy that too?" So remember if you're going to mess with people's heads do it subtly.

The next stage to gaining someone's trust and commitment to your cause is to understand what is important to them and makes them tick. Their drivers may be different to yours but at least you can try and get your head around them.

You don't need to like someone to trust them but it really helps.

Once you've established contact, true commitment is deciding you are going to make the relationship work, throughout the ups and downs and the differences of opinion. It is important that both people have a shared understanding about the basis of the relationship, even about basic things.

"If you don't make mistakes, you're not working on hard-enough problems. And that's a big mistake"

F. Wikzek –
poet

Most misunderstandings and mistrust comes from not having a shared understanding or contract. To students of failure, we recommend any conversation that begins "But I thought..." as this inevitably means a lack of shared commitment. Contracts or agreements make it clear where you both stand and allow you to be your real self. People who have not set clear ways of working or arrangements often feel insecure and feel they can't count on the other person. When people feel secure they often find it easier to get close to others and trust them.

Commitment involves looking out for someone, being a friend and seeing their success and happiness as important as your own. In essence it is about treating the other person with respect. Trust is about knowing the other person will take responsibility and live up to expectations. You can count on them to do the right thing in any situation and you respect their judgement. For a relationship to be healthy trust needs to be reciprocated.

With these wise words echoing around your noggin, we would recommend the services of a website called *fakealibi.co.uk*. The press release for this shrine to relationship failure reads as follows:

> A controversial website offering customers alibis for marital affairs has begun accepting members in the UK.
>
> The founder of fakealibi.co.uk, Rob Mendoza, says he would not use the site personally, but recognises there is a need for assistance in concealing the truth in certain situations in order to assist in saving relationships.
>
> The site was established to help people who cannot avoid infidelity, but want to keep their families intact.

We'd affiliate the college with the chaps who run this site, if only we weren't too busy out philandering ourselves. We love the idea that there are people 'who cannot avoid infidelity'. It's a bit like a person driving along a road who sees he is heading for a tree and resigns himself to hitting it whatever the case. In the case of *fakealibi*, it's actually more like the tree was hiding behind another tree and sneaked up on the victim unawares. This analogy at least gives the guilty party an excuse which is about as flimsy and outrageous as: "It's not my fault, I cannot avoid infidelity."

And while we use a deliberately sexist 'he' in this example, at the last count the gender of the folk using this service was split 60:40, with women only slightly behind in the infidelity stakes.

3 Freedom

In most happy relationships people don't live in each other's pockets. By this we mean financially, obviously. Creating giant trousers to house your partner would be plain absurd and we only go in for sound theory at the College of Failure – however, we digress.

The healthiest and happiest relationships are those where both partners give each other freedom to enjoy life apart from each other. It is important to have friends and activities that you each can enjoy on your own. Freedom in a relationship is allowing each other to keep a sense of self. This is equally true in business – empowerment may be a buzzword, but friends, colleagues and team members need different levels of space, challenge and support. When you're thinking about the amount of freedom to offer another person, remember that space for one person can be another person's agoraphobia.

> **"My downfall raises me to infinite heights"**
> Napoleon Bonaparte – statesman

Freedom is about not expecting the other person to be a clone of yourself. Success means respecting each other's rights to have different opinions, likes and dislikes, and appreciating that just because you want something they may not! Time for reflection and just being alone is also good for healthy relationships. It gives you time to think things through and make changes and dream and plan for the future.

Having digested yet more of the distilled words of successful folk through the ages we return to the *living each other's pockets* analogy. To best illustrate the doctrine of the College that freedom is a no-go area, take a moment to reflect on the old nursery rhyme about the Old Woman. Looking back on it this is a very unpleasant ditty indeed. However, it serves our purposes as far as showing how much freedom you should allow each other goes:

There was on old woman who lived in a shoe
She had so many children she didn't know what to do.
She gave them some broth without any bread,
Then whipped them all soundly
And put them to bed.

4 Friendship and Support

Lasting relationships are built on two people who are friends. Closely linked to friendship is support. Support means helping each other out and sharing responsibilities. In short it is about thinking about the other person as well as yourself. If you can put yourself in the other person's shoes and see what the relationship is like on their side then you can start to see what you both need to be successful. The only time we put ourselves in other's shoes is when we indulge our penchant for tottering around in stilettos now and then, but that is none of your business, frankly.

If you want to get the whole friendship and support thing right, just ask yourself what objections might they have to what you would like to do.

Four tips for great friendships:

- Take the opportunity to learn about the other persons point of view
- Be open to new ideas and ways of doing things
- Accept who you are, you don't need to be better than other people to be liked
- Be open to the feelings and needs of the other person

As you might have guessed we do quite a lot of external consultancy across the globe – that's why the world is in so much of a mess. We are especially fond of our political wranglings. One notable success was in Austria where refusal to offer understanding and support ended in a sword fight.

Heinz-Christian Strache – a member of the far-right Austrian Freedom Party – likened party leader, Joerg Haider, to a "crazy dog barking at the moon". Roman Strassl leapt to his leader's aid, saying Strache had offended the honour of the leader. They argued until 2am at which point Strassl challenged Strache to a duel – as you do. Afterwards the party wouldn't admit who won, but we can only hope this medieval approach to friendship and support spreads; it is a very straight forward way to 'foil' any ambitions of success you might harbour.

"He who never makes mistakes never makes anything"

English Proverb

5   Working at your relationship

Working at any relationship simply means putting effort into the relationship. It is about being interested and thoughtful. It is about turning a blind eye to the things you find annoying and focusing on the things you like, valuing personal differences, working styles and thinking. It also means solving problems before they escalate, and making each other feel special.

One study by Dr Maryon Tysoe showed how this kind of behaviour decreased a year after people made a commitment to each other. The research showed that approval and compliments dropped by 30% and doing something nice for each other dropped 28%. Of course we know you can do better than that, but the folk in that study hadn't had the benefit of our unique tutorial.

For the successful, the trick is to express your delight every time you think something nice. Say thank you as often as possible; that includes things like "thanks for listening" or "thanks for being nice to me when I felt down". The more positive feedback you give the more the other person will continue to be nice to you. We of course will advocate concentrating on the negative, which you will find is remarkably easy. Take this stinker of an example from Sweden.

Computer technician Goran Andervass rebuked an anonymous colleague who he claimed had deliberately broken wind in his office. "My colleague was absolutely aware of the awful smell – it was pure provocation," Mr Andervass said. "I felt provoked by the fart at 7.30am and it made me terribly angry."

Now Mr Andervass made no attempt to consider the situation and launched into a tirade without a thought of turning a blind eye. However, he was outdone by the smelly colleague who reported this behaviour to management who suspended and then made Mr Andervass redundant. Mr Andervass subsequently won £58,000 damages for unfair dismissal, which was the icing on our failure cake.
Everyone ignored the needs of everyone else and everyone lost out. We couldn't have done it better ourselves.

Working at it also means having fun. We all need routine but if you can predict what you will be doing every night of the week for the next month and the next year then things could go horribly wrong.

(Hooray!) It can be pleasant at times knowing what you are going to do, but the rest of the time it can become dull and boring. Take it from us, there is nothing that will grind you down more quickly than doing the same thing again and again, and again, and again, and again, and again, and again, and again, and again, and again, and again, and again, and again, and again.

Oh, and then again.

6 Learn to love yourself

We are getting rather teary-eyed at this point. We're well into our journey of failure together and we're having something of a literary midlife crisis. Having spent some very good quality time together we are in little doubt of our affections towards you. However, this is going to have to suffice as we strongly advise you against loving yourself.

Successful folk know that in any relationship it is important to recognise what you have to offer; your good points – basically what makes you, you.

Consider this, you're in a shop and admiring a new suit you think you'll buy, when a sales assistant comes over.

> *"There is no failure except in not trying"*
> Elbert Hubbard – author

"This is great," you say. "Just what I have been looking for."

"Do you really think so?" they reply. "Actually it is not very well made, the seams are not stitched properly and I think it is over priced."

Are you going to respond by giving your credit card and saying "I'll take it"? You are more likely to walk away thinking "thank goodness I didn't spend my money on that!" It is the same in a relationship, if you don't think you have something to offer how are you going to convince someone else?

So while we have finely tailored this magnum opus to the most important considerations that our students of failure will need, you have to come across like a cheap suit, which appears to have been tailored to a passing stegosaurus.

People can tell from the moment you walk into a room the esteem in which you hold yourself. If this applies to the general public, it becomes obvious that selling yourself becomes nothing short of imperative to the one who is destined to spend their whole life with you – you.

As Oscar Wilde once said: "Learning to love yourself is the beginning of a life long relationship."

With such advice we would have expelled Wilde immediately from the College. Either that or kept him in a cage to amuse us with his ever-constant flow of witticisms. We suppose we'll never know unless we defrost him. (Our next book on cryogenics is going to be a big seller.)

SUCCESS WARNING!

Relationships with yourself and with others will always require work but they are essential to success. Invest time and care and reap the rewards. It will make life more happy and fulfilling than you can imagine if you take time to understand why people act in a certain way.

"Failure calls out for a need to change direction or keep going in the same direction or to stop altogether. But sometimes you have to try each before you hear which one it is"

Dr. Howard Dansky –
psychologist

Coaching Yourself
Reflect on the lessons learned from Beginner Level Failure and fill in the blanks:

Goals
1 ....
2 ....
3 ....

Personal strengths
1 ....
2 ....
3 ....

Immediate challenges/blocks/problems
1 ....
2 ....
3 ....

Development of skills
1 ....
2 ....
3 ....

Achievements
1 ....
2 ....
3 ....

Goals – Make sure your goals are positive and are about the things you want in your life. These can be some of the failure points you want to stop or some of the success points you want to continue or start.

Personal strengths – Look for your strengths, these can include anything from behaviours, skills, values and attitudes.

Immediate challenges/blocks/problems – List here negative things that directly affect you.

Development of skills – The development of skills listed here should be relevant to the goals set and the ones you are looking to develop to achieve your success.

Achievements – List achievements that you are proud of.

Section the Second

Intermediate Failure – Workplace and team-based failure

We've looked at what you can to do yourself to forge forward in the failure stakes. Much of what you've learned already will affect your conduct in the workplace but now we'll look at directly influencing teams and business relationships.

Cultural Awareness

The world is globalising faster than you can say "cultural misunderstanding". If you choose to ignore this then you're heading for failure on a global scale.

In a previous section nattily entitled 'Money, money, money' we suggested you might like to take a few unmerited days off now and again. But if the idea of taking time off sick is a little scary for you (and let's face it, being afraid is one of the building blocks of failure) then you could just be regularly late and claim it is nothing more than a cultural misunderstanding.

In Brazil they believe latecomers are likely to be more successful in business than those who make it on time. This is because these latecomers are presumed to have busier schedules that negate them being on time.

The lesson here is that an understanding – or lack thereof – of cultural differences can be your friend in the quest for failure. If you understand what people from different places expect, then it's easier to let them down. Whatever folk say about the world becoming a 'global village', the number of different customs that remain between countries and even their nearest neighbours is staggering. The smallest amount of effort to understand people from a different culture that you are doing business with will pay dividends.

So as a student of failure, either you can ignore cultural differences (refer to appendix 3 Chevy Nova Awards – The importance of understanding cultural differences) and let the hilarity ensue or you could make yourself aware of other customs so that you don't inadvertently miss opportunities to upset Johnny Foreigner. (This term goes down well *everywhere*, by the way.)

For example, in the Netherlands they reckon you're untrustworthy if you don't turn up on time. With this in mind, wander into meetings with the Dutch as and when you choose.

Or perhaps you'd like to tap your two index fingers together in the presence of Arabs. While your boss thinks you are pensively thinking about the deal, the Arab chaps will be wondering why you are asking them to sleep with you.

There's one final tale of cultural awareness that it would be remiss of us not to share with you. A man from Aberdeen in Scotland was seconded to his company's office in Gabon in West Africa. Now those of you who have been to the north east of Scotland will appreciate the stiff wind that comes off the North Sea.

Obviously missing home, this chap took to breaking his own winds around the office and was soon issued with a formal complaint by his colleagues. He declared that he did it all the time back home and it was fine. His African colleagues responded that he should respect international cultures a bit more and promptly filed the complaint under 'biohazard'.

They say it's a small world, but the lesson here is that it offers numerous avenues that lead to a gratifying dead end should you choose blissful ignorance over being well-informed about the expectations of colleagues or clients.

SUCCESS WARNING!

Understand the organisational and national cultures that make up your work environment. Remember that everyone has different hopes and expectations and these are fuelled by different cultural identities so don't always presume they will think or react the same as you in any given situation. If in doubt – ask.

Schoolyard politics

It's worth noting that a schoolyard mentality can be invaluable to you. Never be seen to be enjoying your work, even if you actually do. Just as when you were a whippersnapper back at school, remember that being seen to enjoy your work means you are bit sad, a teacher's pet or a workaholic. You are way too cool for that. Accept the all-conquering power of peer pressure.

Of course people who make it in business are often those who didn't tow the line of the 'in crowd' at school and are almost always not the ones who sat at the back of the bus causing trouble. In the world of work you can and will be rewarded for hard work and innovative thinking.

As a student of failure if you have to justify the schoolyard mentality to yourself, remember that many years of your life were taken learning the lore of the playground and it's terribly unreasonable for anyone to expect you to move on from that. Why on earth do people call them your formative years if you don't get to show your form once you've finally been released into the community? What's the point in all that 'character building' if your carefully constructed edifice of paranoia, inadequacy and half-baked ideas are allowed to go to wrack and ruin? It's nothing short of criminal.

To successfully carry this off we move swiftly into the realms of the 'them and us' scenario.

SUCCESS WARNING!

Have the strength and courage of your convictions to put your own ideas forward. If there's something wrong take a moment to offer an alternative. All the other party can do is say no. There is nothing cool about doing something just because someone else has deemed it cool.

"Them and us"

There's plenty of the 'them and us' mentality in the workplace so you're going to have to strive hard to stand out. The key here is to totally align yourself with the staff to the detriment of your manager. It's just like being a militant trade union rep without paying the subs. There's nothing like a bad relationship with your manager to turn a glass ceiling into a concrete one.

In our exalted experience the vast majority of managers want to get on with things and are not the monsters of the industrial revolution. They may not communicate this very well (bad communication is a key part of failure in management while we're on the subject), but they usually mean well. If they actually don't mean well then they're probably on the road to failure alongside you.

Successful people realise that if you take the time to talk to the boss there is an awful lot you'll learn about them that will explain their behaviour. For example, did you know that almost half of managers claim they are being bullied from above and below in the organisation?

Research by the UK's Chartered Management Institute found that 39% of all managers have been bullied in the past three years.

Almost half the middle managers (49%) said they had been victims of bullying. Bet you never realised that. Snippets of information like this go a long way to understanding management behaviour and if you can crack that, then you're going to go far.

> *"You may feel disappointed if you fail, but you are doomed if you don't try"*
> Beverly Sills – *opera singer*

All this goes to show that if you want a fast-track to failure you need to remember a single number: 1984. It's You against the Establishment: Big Brother is watching so make George Orwell proud.

For a practical illustration of the kind of adversarial relationship you are looking for let us once again look abroad for enlightenment. Take China, where it has only been a few years since couples had to ask their employers for permission to get married.

As a celebration of the 54th year of Communist rule the government decreed that star-crossed lovers no longer had to have the consent of their 'work unit' to tie the knot. The new law also meant that you could get a passport without the permission of your employer.

While you and I might immediately note there is something a little unfair about these practices, it took an academic in China – one professor Wu Changzhen from the China University of Political Science and Law – to observe: "Some people didn't have a good relationship with their managers, so when they wanted to get permission for marriage they were refused."

There's no need to learn Mandarin, all you (as a representative of the College) have to remember is every manager has the potential to act in this way and they must be stopped. This applies even if you can see the manager's point of view or are actually fool enough agree with it.

SUCCESS WARNING!
Be clear that you need big relationships at all levels of the organisation. Understand and nurture relationships with those in key decision making positions whether they be formal or informal roles. True success comes from aligning your individual goals with the team and organisational goals – remember you are all in it together.

Woof ! Meouw !

The beauty of the venerable study of failure is just how adaptable it is to the personal neuroses of the individual. For if you are not comfortable with being too cool for school or hating your work and your boss, then you can always go the other way and pander to the employer's every need.

As weird as it may be, people can maintain very little respect for those who always do what they are told and who are always on hand to serve their latest whim. Inconsiderate, you might think, yet rather effective in the failure stakes.

The type of animal you choose to model yourself on is up to you, but might we suggest the beagle or poodle – certainly nothing with a commanding presence. The saying goes that 'the meek shall inherit the Earth'.

This may be so, but the metaphysics of the afterlife are none of our concern. In the meantime let the Earth inherit you.

Successful people understand that resilience is key to success and set clear boundaries so they cannot be pushed about and taken advantage of. So, dear student, do as you are told; especially when it seems unreasonable to you.

"My great concern is not whether you failed, but whether you are content with your failure"

Abraham Lincoln –
US president

Never attempt to put any kind of reasoned argument of your own across. Your colleagues might well call you a 'suck up' – but stick with it and flip your industrial cleaning mechanism up to 'max' and soon all the failure that you can suck up will be yours.

Successful people will accept reasonable demands on them and their time but they will be firm if others start to take advantage of their good will. They will neither jump in and accept everything, nor will they turn down anything out of hand. The successes will listen and assess any request upon its merits and circumstances.

We, however, know it is fine just to blurt out the first thing that comes into your tiny little mind. Another management parable from days of yore illustrates this well:

A sales rep, an administration clerk and their manager are walking to lunch when they find an antique oil lamp. They rub it and a genie comes out in a puff of smoke.

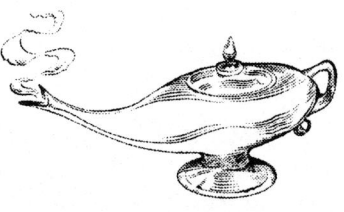

The genie says: "I usually only grant three wishes, so I'll give each of you just one." "Me first! Me first!" cries the admin clerk. "I want to be in the Bahamas, driving a speedboat, without a care in the world." Poof! She's gone.

The sales rep overcomes his astonishment and quickly babbles: "I want to be in Hawaii with my personal masseuse, an endless supply of Pina Coladas and the love of my life!" Poof! He's off too. "Right, your turn," the genie says to the manager.

The manager looks the genie up and down and says: "I want those two back in the office as soon as lunch is over." The moral of the story: it might be worth listening carefully what your boss has to say first before you jump in.

SUCCESS WARNING!

Saying no, within reason is acceptable. Challenging as well as supporting your boss/peers is right. Be clear on your priorities. She/he

will respect someone far more who tells them what they need to hear rather than what they want to hear. (Please note the amount of challenge, style and type will be dependent on the boss and the culture of the organisation).

Hard times

The next option is for those of you looking for a real challenge. We're talking about the ones who can't help but be committed and who work hard. To fail with this particular approach takes real dedication so strap yourself in and here we go.

There is a maxim in the success community that you should dress for the job that is two above the position you currently hold. You can apply this on a more general basis and ask: "What will I need for the next job I want?"

Such vision is strictly forbidden at the College of Failure as aspiration is a clear route to success. The student of failure realises he or she should only focus on their current role, never look for the next step and what it would take to get up the career ladder. As the superstitious failures among us know ladders – even career ones – should be walked underneath for maximum impact.

So work your little cotton socks off if you like but be sure to consider your current job as the only job in the world. Stand still and grow stagnant.

Let the algae of failure cover you and make you smell of disappointment. (As soon as we've worked out how to bottle this particular fragrance we shall take the fashion world by storm. Our slogan will be: *Failure: because you are not worth it.*)

> *"Use the losses and failures of the past as a reason for action not inaction"*
>
> Charles J Given – lawyer

Staying stuck in a rut is actually simpler than it might sound. If you combine an unwillingness to address the next step in your career with the Shrinking Violet technique mentioned at the start of the book then it could become decidedly easy.

There's two reasons for this. One: no one wants to promote anyone into any area of responsibility if they are akin to a wet lettuce. Two: anyone who works as hard as you is likely to be irreplaceable and no manager in their right mind wants to be off recruiting to replace you – the *uber*-employee. Combine these two and your fight to remain stationary will be unstoppable.

SUCCESS WARNING!

Take a long term view, weight up the options and look at how they might fit in with your next career move. Then ask yourself: "is this taking me towards where I want to go?" Always be on the lookout for opportunity and seize it when it arises. If you don't, then someone else will.

We need a volunteer

Clearly you need to be very sure that you never, ever volunteer for anything. Successful people understand that volunteering for the right things will speed them on their way. To avoid this, ask yourself the following questions:

- Will volunteering enable me to learn and develop?
- Will it enable me to work with people that would be great to work with or who will enhance my performance?

If the answer is yes to either of these questions then head for the hills.

Paying heed to these simple questions will ensure that eventually no one will ever ask you anything. In fact start as you mean to go on – if someone asks you to do something be totally clear and even rude if necessary and confirm you are far too busy to take on any more work. Do this even if it is a perfectly reasonable request and one that is likely to shower you in praise. To cut a long story short, never volunteer; it's just too risky.

If, for some unfathomable reason, you feel the urge to volunteer adopt the same process of asking yourself how this will help you and then make sure the returns are minimal if not downright dangerous to your person. Working towards something that is of no benefit to you at all is a delightful method of speeding you on your way to failure.

Have you ever heard tales of the Forlorn Hope? They were the groups of soldiers during the Napoleonic period who would be first into the breach of shattered walls of big fortresses. They tended to volunteer because if they were successful then they'd get more money and promotions. Sadly most of them tended to get blown to pieces.

This is an example of when you might like to volunteer as the odds of success are so heavily stacked against you that failure is almost inevitable.

> *"Many men fail because they quit too soon"*
> Dr. C E Welch – entrepreneur

However, it's always better to just go the whole hog and refuse to volunteer. What would happen if you did volunteer and – however unexpectedly – things went right and showed you in a positive light? This would devalue the efforts of every hard working student of failure and would demean all their hard lost successes. When you look at it that way, volunteering is just plain selfish. You should be ashamed of yourself.

SUCCESS WARNING!

Ask yourself the following questions: will volunteering enable me to learn and develop my skills, knowledge and experience? Will it enable me to work with people that would be great to work with or who will enhance my performance?

If the answer is yes then get involved.

In for a penny...

Another alternative which is equally successful in the failure stakes is to volunteer for everything.

The great Bill Cosby once said: "The key to failure is to please everybody". Maybe this was an excuse to placate all the people who didn't find him funny. We like to think that he was pushing for honorary membership of the College of Failure with his nuggets of wisdom. Perhaps we shall never know.

Volunteering for everything will ensure you are not valued, you are over-worked and the dogsbody everyone gives the work they don't want to do. The knock on effect will be you don't have time to do the stuff you've already got thus resulting in a domino failure effect.

And this is not the only benefit. The experience you get from all these projects is invaluable – it will enable you to recognise a mistake when you make it again.

SUCCESS WARNING!

Volunteer strategically; ask yourself what are the benefits for me in volunteering? What will I lose if I do not? In relation to my long term plan how does it help? What impact will it have on my relationships or the goodwill of others? What is the reason for this person wanting someone to do this?

Reading the Small Print

Successful people know that there's no point in promising the world if you can't deliver it. If you take on too much then inevitably someone will be disappointed. As you might have guessed, our unswerving opinion on this matter is that you should always over-promise and under-deliver.

If someone wants a piece of work as soon as possible and you know realistically it will take five days, tip your head jauntily to the side and declare that it will take a day. The great news is they will be really happy to hear you are going to deliver much faster than anyone else and faster than they thought possible. Ha ha! More fool them!

Throughout this day it might be nice to offer periodic updates – over-exaggerated of course – thus creating a suitable environment for maximum disappointment when the hammer falls come deadline time. When they get angry because you have not delivered on time and declare that they no longer trust you

"Failures are the finger posts on the road to achievement"

Charles F Kettering –
inventor

this is a good time just to sit back and take a moment to revel in their discomfort. There's nothing wrong with letting the misery of your colleagues – especially when caused by oneself – wash over you for a moment.

Once you have basked in the warm glow of others' discomfort for a while, gear up and make it clear that it was not your fault, it took longer than expected and it is *soooo* unfair. This just adds another layer of dishonesty to the mix – a trifle of lies and disappointment, if you will.

The invention of the email has created a wealth of examples upon which we may draw. The following offer is one that you might like to take as a foundation for any promises you make in the office in future. Like your promises, one has the feeling that this might be something of a con. It is reproduced almost as received – the only thing we have changed is the company details since they'd nicked another business' details, expecting people to believe this nonsense:

> Hello!
>
> *The company on development web project are required Financial Leader(permanent or temporary work). You it is necessary whole only pair of hours a day for this work, rest we shall teach you. The company guarantees the social package, honesty in cooperation, ensuring the salary beforehand on acceptance on work, vacation. Acceptance is realised on competitive base. We are pleased each workman!*
>
> Salary from £5,000 in mounth.

SUCCESS WARNING!

Under-promise and over-deliver. If you are working on a project, give regular updates on progress and success and early warning signs on possible problematic issues. Communication is vital; it will build trust and reassurance. People like to know where they stand as it enables them to prepare contingencies, so do not be afraid of telling them how the land lies.

Tip the work-life balance

We've already talked about how important volunteering for everything can be in your quest for failure. Having mastered said approach, it's time to build on this until there is nothing in your life but work.

Despite what all the do-gooders say you don't need a work-life balance. While successful people realise that there was never any law made about life having to be serious, we at the College take this matter very seriously indeed.

There's a mass of research to suggest that attaining a good work-life balance is a prerequisite for success. That is why we avoid it like the plague.

> *"I have always grown from my problems and challenges, from the things that don't work out. That's when I've really learned"*
> Carol Burnett – comedienne

Repeat this mantra: 'I can work myself into the ground and still reach peak performance' – preferably when lying in bed after you were tempted to snatch a few hours shut-eye out of the office, you slacker!

If you need convincing just how important tipping this balance is then don't listen to us, try some other boffins for size. A recent study in the US showed that overtime is really rather bad for you. What great news! There's nothing to gladden the heart of a student of failure quite like a positive statistic like that. It is a veritable signpost to inadequacy – as long as you take the right track, obviously. The survey found that staff who work overtime were 61% more likely to become hurt or ill. Working more than 12 hours a day raised the risk by more than a third, according to the University of Massachusetts. This is backed up by recent research from clever folk at the McKinsey consultancy who worked out that managers at the world's most successful companies work on average one hour longer than anyone else. They work smarter, not harder. You must avoid this behaviour at all costs.

If that's not enough to persuade you of the validity of work-life balance let's look at it from a national perspective. The UK has the second longest average working hours in Europe (behind Poland), yet the UK languishes behind all it's major competitors – France, Germany, Scandinavia – in the productivity of its workers.

Remember the old idiom – 'there's no place like home'? Well in the modern age, dear student of failure, home is where the heart is – and that is firmly planted together with your buttocks on the chair in your office.

Here at the College we consider sleep just a form of industrial action masquerading under a different name. It must be stamped out.

SUCCESS WARNING!
Seek a work-life balance. Sustainable high performance comes from being a rounded, balanced person. It makes you more interesting, happier and you live longer. Excessive hours at work lead to sickness and accidents, not success.

Client, shmi-ent

Forget what is important to your clients, do what is important to you. If they're foolish enough to lavish vast sums on you then so be it. Remember from earlier teachings: you know best. Whoever said the client is always right was never a fellow of our college, we can tell you.

Remember your client may be another company or body or it may be the line manager for whom you are doing a piece of work. Whoever it is, follow your own agenda and remember when the bell goes it's time to go home. The Romans used to say 'tempus fugit' – time flies (when you are having fun). We recommend 'failus fugit' – the student of failure flies (out the door when 5.30 comes round).

Never go the extra mile otherwise you will be remembered for the right things, God forbid. It's much easier to be remembered for doing the wrong things – poor service alone will make you infamous.

Take the example of Danish vicar, Torkild Gorsboll, who turned to his congregation and admitted he thought God 'was no more real the Robin Hood'. Now you'd think his congregation would be

"If you have tried to do something and failed, you are vastly better off than if you had tried nothing and succeeded"

Richard Martin Stern – *novelist*

taken aback at this, as indeed they probably were. However, he shocked them further by adding that resurrection and eternal life were also stretching things a bit, in his opinion.

This blatant affront to those who he served illustrates just how effective ignoring your client base can be. But make sure you hold your ground – Torkild recanted his admission after being suspended and was given his post back.

SUCCESS WARNING!

Establish what your client's needs are. Ask them what is important to them. Then deliver what the client wants. If you go the extra mile you will surprise people and in turn you will build your reputation. Do the unexpected if you can link it to the needs and goals of your client, whoever they may be.

The apparel oft proclaims the man

Would sir or madam kindly like to step this way? It is time to tailor your appearance for your odyssey of inadequacy. Oh dear, we seem to have the measuring tape behind – no matter, it was only to be used to tie round your waist as a belt anyway. We'll just let your trousers fall down shall we?

Take a moment to observe the dress code and style of those highly successful people in your organisation as this will tell you – the student of failure – what to stay away from. They tend to have that 'sharp dresser' kind of look. You know the one – where creases seem to shy away from their clothing as if they are surrounded by a force-field of freshly-pressed confidence. If these folk are said to 'look the part', then it would be wise for you to look *a* part, but a part of something else altogether.

So if it is a smart working environment then ripped jeans, trainers, mini-skirts, your favourite Hawaiian shirt and sun glasses are key. There's nothing like a scruffy appearance to inspire a lack of confidence in others in a smart office environment. Of course if you worked in a surf shop on the beach then we say put that suit on immediately.

Anything that you deem out of keeping from the ethos of the office will suffice – just look to the bottom half of your laundry basket for inspiration. This season might we also recommend sir or madam tries using the ungroomed look with a 'just got out of bed and sweaty motif'? Delightful.

They say that for success you should dress for the position you want in two jobs time. For failure the rule is you should dress for the pub or night club you plan to be in in two *hours* time.

But don't trust us on this. Recent research from the Federal Reserve Bank of St Louis in the US, showed that people who look more attractive have a tendency to make more money and get promoted quicker than the bedraggled mess that crawled out of your bed this morning.

They found there was 'plainness penalty' of 9% in wages but a 'beauty premium' of 5% in pay if you looked good – so all those sharp dressers are actually making their money back.

It's important to consider the approach from the ground up. A survey by recruitment agency Connections in the North West of England found that 70% of interviewers noticed and judged potential recruits by their footwear. This is a long established trait which is in fact based in pop music, we have discovered.

Remember back in 1966 when Nancy Sinatra sang: "These boots are made for working and that's just what I'll do. One of these days these boots are going to work all over you." Wise words indeed.

> *"Good people are good because they've come to wisdom through failure. We get very little wisdom from success, you know"*
>
> William Saroyan – *author*

Despite being a mere shred of polyester/rayon mix, ties can also be very helpful to you if they happen to be part of the office uniform. Step back into our fitting room while we offer you this fine range of animal print and cartoon character emblazoned ties. Would sir or madam be interested in our extensive of range of musical ties?

They can also be useful on the legal front. In 2003 in the UK a member of staff at Jobcentre Plus decided to take the government to court because he was forced to wear a tie. He said it was discrimination as the women in the office didn't have to wear them. Unbelievably he won. So we put out an all areas call to your fellow students, who lodged employment tribunal applications in their thousands, thus annoying their managers on a national scale with their use of clothing. Inspiring stuff.

SUCCESS WARNING!
First impressions count and last. The old age saying of "dress to impress" is vital. Visual stimuli can be much more powerful – and certainly more memorable than the spoken word. A picture is worth a thousand words so make sure you are a masterpiece and not just graffiti.

Feel the pain of branding

Personal brand is not just about what the individual wears and the visual image that they present. It is also about the impression that the individual presents through the way that they behave, the way and manner in which they talk as well as through their body language.

If we asked you to come up with three words that come into your mind when you think of Richard Branson they might include 'entrepreneurial', 'creative' and 'unconventional'. He himself has become a brand in the same way as Coca Cola or Pepsi is a brand.

Think what three words a colleague would apply to you – and be honest. Better still go and ask them now. Now set yourself three words that you would like to be applied to you. Then dress, behave and interact with people, always bearing in mind what these three things are. Soon it will become second nature.

If we asked an associate of yours for the first three things that came to mind if they described you in business terms to someone else, what would they say? Boring, lazy and a no-hoper would be a great start for a star of failure. Equally impressive would be confrontational, big-headed and arrogant. Choose your three words carefully as they are the difference between being Donald Trump and Donald the Tramp.

SUCCESS WARNING!

We all have a personal brand and every conversation or meeting is a chance to either enhance or detract from your brand. Focus on what you are and what you want to become. Just three words will provide this focus.

"Failure is the tuition you pay for success"

Walter Brunell –
writer

Questions, questions, questions...

Questions are never the answer. As you have previously learned, you risk irritating bouts of success if you seek the insight of others. However, this does not mean you have to shun the company of others.

If, like many of us here at the College, you are something of a philanthropist, then you will need to share your worldly wise words (try saying that after a couple of brandies!) So talk, talk, talk and talk as much as possible but what ever happens avoid listening. That will put you back on the route to learning, and we can't have that. If you find yourself on the wrong end of a conversation and are not speaking then simply interrupt. If by some freak accident or other there is no way to break their interminable prose then simply switch off and don't listen.

Listening, absorbing and challenging is the only way to gain new knowledge and expertise. You may value your own opinion but you can't improve yourself only by looking inwards. That's why successful folk are inquisitive and no matter how successful they are, are always ready to listen, if only so they can steal your ideas.

Finer proponents of the art of *refusing* to pay attention will find themselves finishing people's sentences and true experts will actually ask questions such as: "Are you going on holiday this year"? to further their own diatribe: "Oh you are – I am going to Florida myself..."

You'd be very surprised how much can be learned with the simple art of listening. Avoid it at all costs. Instead follow pop star Madonna's wisdom when she said: "Listen, everyone is entitled to my opinion".

SUCCESS WARNING!

Questions are the answer. As the saying goes: first seek to understand and only then to be understood. Communication is vital – ask questions and listen; the answers on how to influence, motivate and lead are all there for the taking. It is a very rare person who will not share their knowledge and wisdom with you if you ask.

Mentor? Mental, more like!

Beware the baleful influence of a mentor. Highly successful and effective people often have mentors, coaches and friends that challenge, support and give advice. These are individuals who are often leaders in their chosen field.

If you have chosen them wisely, they will help you if you only take the opportunity to ask. Their experience can be invaluable to successful people. Mentors can be a mine of information. However, this is a mine that you need to close quicker than Margaret Thatcher could in the 1980's. Never take on a mentor who you can go to for help, advice or support.

But beware the hidden mentor! (Cue crash of lightening and scary keyboard effects...) They don't have to be heads of corporations, world-beating athletes or even the writers of amusing, yet ultimately informative books. They can be anyone who knows their stuff and is willing to share. You'd be surprised how often people will share the knowledge you need if you do but ask. If they don't then there's every chance they're studying the fine art of failure as diligently as you.

> *"Believe and act as if it is impossible to fail"*
>
> Charles F Kettering – *inventor*

To avoid any risk of finding yourself coupled to a mentor, get it into your head that asking will be seen as a sign of weaknesses. (Of course refusing to ask questions is actually a sign of either fear or pigheadedness, but we'll gloss over that.)

The road to failure is a long and lonely one with only us and the voices in your head to keep you company. Sorry, that's just the way it's got to be – we're sure you understand.

SUCCESS WARNING!
Highly successful and effective people often have mentors, coaches and friends who they can learn from and go to for advice. They will offer information, reassurance and compassion or might just ask the right questions and listen. When the going gets tough this is just what you will need to succeed.

Fist impressions last

First impressions count. They're a pivotal part of establishing your lack of prowess from the get-go and can put the student of failure valuable steps behind the opposition before you've even muttered one ill-chosen word.

It's important to note that the first impression begins before you might have even seen a person. This might happen across a room or deck (for the seafarers among you, or rather those of you who are all at sea).

Start by making sure you negate any chance of a good first impression by never smiling. A simple smile will put others at ease and this will in turn do the same for you. A scowl – or a good gurn if you can – will start things off on the wrong foot.

Having come within stroking distance of a person, the first 10 seconds are vital. Let's start with the handshake.

Key techniques:-

1. If you are strong impose yourself using 'the crusher' – make a literal impression on them by breaking every bone in their hands and stopping the blood supply.

2. Hardly touch them – shake hands like

a wet lettuce with just the ends of your finger. The only successful people who get away with this are heads of state and they do it so they don't get trapped in the clutches of some deranged voter/assassin.

3   Finally, for all you hip and trendy people, 'high five' any new acquaintances and anyone more senior than you in the office. They will love it and probably shout "Yo!" or some other example of urban parlance in return. "Word up to one's homies," as the MD might say.

Research has shown the most effective handshake for failure purposes is the limp-wristed approach. A recruitment agency called Marketing Professionals 'monitored 200 handshakes' and found one in five men and an impressive 46% of women shook hands like a wet fish.

> *"The only true failure lies in the failure to start"*
> Harold Blake Walker – author

A quarter of men went for the bone crushing approach compared to only 6% of women. When they asked employers which was the most despicable approach they said the softly, softly handshake from potential recruits was the one most likely to put them off hiring them. You know what to do. Go to it.

Next we move on to blurting out the most inappropriate conversation you can possibly manage in the circumstances. A good first line can mark you out as whatever you want to be. At the College of Failure we recommend you put yourself forward as a downright idiot, perhaps using one or two of the following carefully chosen witticisms:

"Fiction writing is great, you can make up almost anything."

Ivana Trump, on finishing her first novel

"I can't really remember the names of the clubs that we went to."

Shaquille O'Neal, basketball player, on whether he had visited the Parthenon during his visit to Greece

"Our enemies are innovative and resourceful, and so are we. They never stop thinking about new ways to harm our country and our people, and neither do we."

President George W. Bush, August 2004

"If history repeats itself, I should think we can expect the same thing again."

        Football manager **Terry Venables**

"I think there is a world market for maybe five computers."

        Thomas Watson, chairman of IBM, 1943

"The lead car is absolutely unique, except for the one behind it which is identical."

        Murray Walker, sportscaster

Now we need to make sure that you continue this disastrous meeting by being the most smarmy, unattractive individual you can. London's *Evening Standard* newspaper did some research into what makes someone a charmer (rather than a smarmer) and we present their findings:

How to be a charmer:

Always:
- laugh at other people's jokes
- tell stories against yourself
- give up your seat to someone more needy
- thoroughly research any intended victim of your charm
- let others talk about themselves
- let people finish their sentences
- play games with your friends' children
- pour the drinks
- pay quietly

Never:
- name drop
- look over other people's shoulders when talking to them
- be overtly drunk
- give advice when it's not asked for
- talk about money
- appear to have made too much effort with your appearance
- assume you are charming
- lunge at a man or women you find attractive. Ever.

> *"The only time you don't fail is the last time you try anything – and it works"*
> William Strong –
> us politician

Of course as a student of failure you need to turn this on its head. Drink enough to make a whale jealous, show everyone your spanking new platinum-lined credit card and lunge like an Olympic swimmer taking to the pool. This swimming analogy also allows us to make jokes about breast stroke, which is also found to be intrusive for some reason.

SUCCESS WARNING!
A firm handshake is vital in any first impression. Also make sure you're then armed with conversation that fits the occasion or audience you have just been introduced to. Remember, people decide within the first 10 seconds if a person is approachable or credible.

Failure: a team game for all ages

It might seem odd to be discussing the potential for failure available to you through the medium of teams. We have stressed on several occasions the need to go it alone and refuse the advice of others. Such an approach lends itself to solitary action and it remains the most effective route to failure.

But however dedicated you might be to the Cause of Failure, some things just happen that are outside your control. This might mean you end up in a team, through no fault of your own, or you could even be put in charge. For these reasons it is important to pay heed to using a team to your own disadvantage.

Let's assume for one blood curdling moment that you have been put in charge. Now you'll need to select the right team. You have two main choices. Number one: develop people with exactly the same style, personality type skills and knowledge as you.

"Surely not!" you cry. "Such wedded bliss can only lead to success, surely?" Not so. By doing this you can ensure you have a team that will make the same mistakes as you and will fail quickly, time and time again. It's a bit like being the despotic leader of some tinpot regime somewhere. They inevitably surround themselves with people who think the same (or if they don't, certainly won't admit it) and decide they are set for a thousand year reign.

Fortunately these folk usually end up failing on a grand scale and their remains scattered through out the land – serve them right too.

The second option open to you is to take the belief there is strength in diversity (which indeed there is). This sort of team will offer you a spectrum of different views, opinions and skills to a different level.

Again you might regard us aghast, wondering where the method to this madness might lie.

> "Failure is, in a sense, the highway to success"
>
> John Keats – poet

As a student of failure choose people who will offer destructive opinions and deliberately choose team members you dislike; the ones who rub you up the wrong way and have values that are violently at odds with yours. This will mean you fail to harness any of the potential within your team.

Of course a successful person will realise that it is nigh on impossible to pick a team of folk who will always agree. However, they will take steps to ensure disagreements are directed towards constructive criticism. Successful people will assuage worries with fact-based evidence and everyone will be made to feel that they have had a fair crack of the whip.

You on the other hand can use disagreements like a wrecking ball to smash people and their egos to pieces. Play people off against one another for fun, take sides and encourage team members to humiliate individuals if they offer ideas that are out of the ordinary. Better still: humiliate anyone who offers any new ideas at all. This is your team, not theirs! Make it clear that they should act like a team and do it your way.

In the interest of knowing your enemy here is a list of things that make up a high performance team so you can be sure to avoid them, based on the work of Douglas McGregor in his book *The Human Side of Enterprise*:

Characteristics of a High Performance Team

1. Clear purpose (defined and accepted vision, mission, goal or task and an action plan)
2. Informality (informal, relaxed and comfortable)
3. Participation (much discussion and everyone encouraged to participate)
4. Listening (members use effective listening techniques such as questioning, paraphrasing and summarising)
5. Civilised disagreement (team is comfortable with disagreement, does not avoid, smooth over or suppress conflict)
6. Consensus decision making (substantial agreement through discussion, avoidance of voting)
7. Open communications (feelings are legitimate, few hidden agendas, not a blame culture)
8. Clear roles and work assignments (clear expectations and work evenly divided)
9. Shared leadership (while there is a formal leader, everyone shares in effective leadership behaviours)
10. External relations (the team pays attention to developing outside relationships, resources, credibility)
11. Style diversity (team has a broad spectrum of group process and skills)
12. Self-assessment (the team periodically stops to examine how well it is functioning)

> *"Sometimes a noble failure serves the world as faithfully as a distinguished success"*
> Edward Dowden – poet

World class teams have a strong commitment to each others' growth and success which distinguishes them from all teams. Energised by this extra commitment they have a deeper sense of purpose, more ambitious performance goals, more complete approaches and mutual accountability.

This tends to lead to a sickening amount of

inter-changeable as well as complementary skills. Of course we only tell you this so you know what to avoid, so use this knowledge wisely.

SUCCESS WARNING!
There is strength in diversity. A successful team will offer you a spectrum of different views, opinions and skills. One individual's strengths will underpin and then support the weaknesses of the others and visa versa. These teams are generally more creative, innovative and achieve higher results.

Relationships on the sea of failure

In the world of success building relationships are key. This being the case, make sure you draw every bolt and latch to ensure this key can open no doors for you. Every now and again you hear stories of people who have 'gone it alone' and who are rabid successes in their chosen field. What is not mentioned is the failures who lie strewn around them — they are the lonely martyrs to our cause.

As always you should be aware that fate has an annoying habit of refusing to play by the rules. There's every chance you might find yourself in a room where over-anxious folk are determined to network with you.

Perhaps you are particularly daring and want to network just for bedevilment. Either way, the student of failure will make sure make sure his or her networking is as superficial as possible. Make sure the net in your network is as full of holes as it can be — the type of net that would let a blue whale pass blithely through. If there's a buffet head towards it as fast your failing feet will carry you. It's difficult to network if you're spitting chewed up vol-au-vents across the room.

Successful types are attuned to when they are confronted with someone who could be of use to them or to whom they might be of some use. This tends to lead to the building of relationships that are mutually beneficial. It's quite simple to spot these people.

Just ask yourself "is there some way I can help or be of use to this person?" and only then ask if they have the knowledge, abilities or even character traits that could help you.

So treat your business cards like confetti and throw them about in a suitably self-important manner. With any luck they'll end up in the hands of people who will merely impede your progress. If you're really lucky they'll end up on a couple of databases that will bombard you with useless information. However, not all of us are that fortunate.

This lesson applies in any social situation. Never socialise with colleagues or other people – they could get to know you and even like you. The thought of that happening is almost unbearable.

SUCCESS WARNING!

Successful types either already know or soon find out if they are confronted with someone who they might be of some use to or whom could be of use to them. This tends to lead to the building of relationships that are mutually beneficial. The word relationship implies a two-way exchange so make sure you are not taking everything and giving nothing back. This in turn builds trust. However, remember not to dismiss or be rude to those that you don't want to network with. This will do your reputation no good at all.

> *"I failed over and over in my life... That is why I succeed."*
> Michael Jordan – *sportsman*

A word in their ears

Your aim in this lesson is to foster an environment of distrust and secrecy that would be more at home in Cold War Eastern Europe than in your office. This way you will never get a chance to explain why relationships are breaking down in the office and will never be able to start constructive dialogues that would resolve problems.

Sadly there are examples from a far more modern time than post-war Eastern Europe that illustrate this point all too well. In post-millenium Eastern Europe in fact. Employers in Serbia are increasingly using lie detectors to check whether or not staff are on the straight and narrow. Employees are finding themselves on the receiving end of questions like: "Do you like your boss" and "Are you loyal to the company?"

The Serbian general workers union has called the trend "an outrageous invasion of privacy" while providers of this delightful service say they provide an invaluable service in ensuring employee loyalty.

Now we aren't for one second recommending a return to the old Communist ways – if only because people were far too scared to risk being a failure back then and that rather leaves us at a loss. However, it does illustrate – albeit in a rather extreme manner – that breeding distrust can be a key demotivator.

So if a colleague does something wrong, we want to see you banging on the boss's door as fast as your little feet can carry you. It's amazing just how many people are too scared to enquire of their immediate colleague why something went wrong and what they are going to do about it. However, they will rush to their superior, cap in hand, to tell tales without any qualms.

More often than not you'll find the wrong-doer will not appreciate the impact of their own failing on you or the team and will be more than eager to help if you would only ask. As they say, ignorance is bliss.

To illustrate this we turn to the Lemur monkey (obviously!) A study of 1,500 staff by recruitment firm Office Angels found this brand of primate is the one that most closely resembles the majority of office folk. The recruitment firm asked the people to define their characters and then got behavioural expert Judi James to match these to animals in the office jungle that behave in similar ways.

52% came out as Lemurs: they were likeable, friendly, hung around in groups and were generally positive about things. They also reported they took pride in what they do. So you see, people are more likely than not to respond to you if you give them the chance.

A bit further down the chain came the koalas who prefer eating or sleeping to hard work (28% of respondents). Now that's more our style. These were closely followed by the elephants who are happy plodding along and tend to dislike change (15%) and hyenas who were loners who liked to keep things close to their chests (5%).

Other animals we might recommend you ape (touché!) are the three-toed sloth to aid your get-up-and-go, the caterpillar for sheer dynamism and the cow, because it releases a lot of wind. This is both anti-social and really rather funny.

> *"The greatest failure is a person who never admits that he can be a failure"*
> Gerald N Weiskott – *leadership guru*

SUCCESS WARNING!

One of the greatest reasons for failings in the workplace is the presumption that people think like you and know what you know. Often something that a colleague does that drives you mad is totally unintentional and could be rectified with a quick word in their ear. Successful people go to the source of the issue and have the conversations that others fear to have.

"You expect me to talk?" "No, Mr Bond, I expect you to fail..."

We feel fairly safe in the assumption that you are not James Bond or any such similar daredevil secret agent. This means you'll happily ignore confidential agreements and tell people inappropriate information without us having to attach electrodes to your extremities.

Having a big mouth is important to the student of failure. We have talked about betraying the inadequacies of your colleagues to your bosses but this doesn't necessarily mean you'll be considered unreliable when it comes to keeping your own information safe. The most despicable person can still be successful if they are seen to be a safe haven for important company and personal information.

If your boss can trust you to keep a secret then he or she can basically entrust you with the deepest (and with any luck most depraved) company secrets. The obvious solution for you is to haemorrhage information ASAP.

This habit is much more popular than you might think. A survey undertaken for an Infosecurity Europe conference found that almost three-quarters of workers were willing to give away the details of their computer password in exchange for a measly chocolate bar. Researchers were interrogating busy commuters at London's Liverpool Street Station, right in the middle of the city's financial district. Should you be a budding hacker, the most common password categories were family names, football teams and pets. The most popular was the devastatingly original 'admin'.

SUCCESS WARNING!
Confidentiality and reliability are fundamental to success. Understand the importance of knowledge and information and how it is used. If you can present yourself as someone trustworthy to your colleagues and superiors you will inevitably be entrusted with ever-greater responsibility.

It's good to talk

You might have noticed that communication with staff/clients/pets or whoever your company is on speaking terms with is becoming more and more noticeable. There are intranets, extranets and adverts everywhere – in fact anything individuals and companies can do to get their message across.

The thing is a lot of the time it still doesn't work very well, which is excellent for our purposes because communication is vital to success. Research by a consultancy called CHA found that 42% of employees think their employer is a poor communicator, while 60% doubt their organisation knows where it is going.

The great irony to all this is that a lack of communication means employers – as well as the colleagues around you – probably think that their communication skills are top notch and that they are as transparent as...well, something very transparent indeed.

> *"To succeed means that you may have to step out of line and march to the sound of your own drummer"*
>
> Keith DeGreen – actor

Methods are put in place to transfer vast quantities of data but little is done by individuals to check whether or not they are getting their message across.

Here's our brief guide to good communication so you can make sure to avoid it:

1 – Work out what you want to say, why you want to say it and who is the lucky recipient of your chatter.

2 – Work out how you are going to relay your wisdom and what format would best suit your audience. For example, they might suffer from hippopotomonstrosesquippedaliaphobia, which, a tad surprisingly, means a fear of long words.

3 – Check what method of relay suits the situation best. For the utmost chance of failing we recommend emailing everything – especially bad news. We find that email is especially well received if the person sits on the desk next to you. This is a surprisingly successful technique for the student of failure. A recent survey by recruitment firm Office Angels found being emailed by the person close enough to actually whisper the message was the number one office peeve.

The top five were:

1. Emailing as just described.
2. Listening to voicemail on speakerphone
3. Swearing at your computer
4. Playing obnoxious radio music
5. People who don't share tea-making duties

Being able to communicate successfully is not that difficult. All it takes is a little time and effort (of which the good student of failure obviously has neither). If you take the time to know what you are talking about there's not an awful lot that can go wrong. At the other end of the scale, a lack of communication leaves people unprepared and out of the loop. Veritable music to our ears.

And it reflects in people's general demeanour and willingness to communicate further. Look around and ask yourself what the people around you need and want. Can you tell? If you can't then they aren't communicating properly and neither are you. Well done indeed.

Now up the ante and try getting up in front of a large group of people and trying to get your message across. Scared? Well so you should be. A poll taken recently found 42% of people in the UK feared public speaking more than losing their job, flying and even death.

We suppose at least you can't be called by Death and told of your impending demise in the same way that fateful telephone calls (or emails!) inform you that at 9.30am, Monday morning you are giving a presentation. Perhaps if Death had such an e-communication tool he might encourage a little more respect from people.

"I honestly think it is better to be a failure at something you love than to be a success at something you hate"

George Burns – comedian

SUCCESS WARNING!
Invest time in communicating, understanding and planning. Remember humans were designed to communicate face to face. Use technology appropriately when it enhances or aids communication not as the only form.

Lies, damned lies and statistics

Linking very closely to our lesson on ethical avoidance (see *Advanced Failure*) is the art of lying. Some will say that honesty is the best policy – not for our purposes it isn't. If you are ever involved in misbehaviour or even just make a mistake, never ever admit it. Even if the facts are there and plain to see – lie, lie, lie, blame someone else, cover it up. Basically do whatever it takes.

When successful people get into a trouble or make a mistake they realise that things can only get worse if it is not rectified. It takes courage to admit you are wrong. The philosopher that said "to err is human..." really hit the nail on the head. He might have done the decent thing and finish it with "but to admit it, divine" because then this example would be much more appropriate, but hay-ho, you can't have everything.

People appreciate honesty and while they might be miffed, or even temporarily mad at you, it will always come back to the age-old quote: "I'm just glad we caught it in time." This is known as damage limitation. Our teachings prefer to ignore damage limitation and stick to limitless damage.

> *"An inventor fails 999 times and if he succeeds once, he's in. He treats his failures simply as practice shots"*
> Charles F Kettering – *inventor*

Moreover, we can prove that lying is a noble thing for you to do, O student of failure. For a long time the fine art of lying has been in decline and it is up to you to carry the torch. The truly lamentable state of lying was outlined by Mark Twain in an essay as far back as 1882 entitled 'On the decay of the art of lying'.

Important excerpts include:

"No high-minded man, no man of right feeling, can contemplate the lumbering and slovenly lying of the present day without grieving to see a noble art so prostituted...

"No fact is more firmly established than that lying is a necessity of our circumstances – the deduction that it is then a virtue goes without saying. No virtue can reach its highest usefulness without careful and diligent cultivation."

But don't think is a task to be undertaken lightly. As Twain says: "An awkward, unscientific lie is often as ineffectual as the truth."

It has been suggested to us that Twain did not actually believe that lying was the done thing and this was merely a clever argument laced with irony. We reject this out of hand and take everything at face value – as you should.

But you are not alone in the quest for unthruth. There are dedicated folk who are working hard to keep the art alive. Take Neville Young, who sailed the seven seas as a senior officer or captain on a number ships before being rumbled as a total fraud.

Young, from Aberdeen in Scotland, carried with him just a forged photocopy of a US Chief Mates Certificate of Competence and faked copies of British and Liberian certificates of competence as he sailed the eight seas (did you notice our cunning lie there? Just something to get you going.)

Of course he was arrested but not until he had been sailing around the globe for five years. Nine months in prison subsequently sank his sailing career without a trace.

SUCCESS WARNING!

When successful people get into trouble or make a mistake they realise that things can only get worse if it is not rectified. It takes courage to admit you are wrong but no one has ever said "I'm glad we caught that later rather than earlier".

Gossip is great – or so we have been told

So we've discussed (in a sort of one-sided printed book kind of way) the importance of lying to failure. This is closely followed by gossip, which is a sanitised version of the lie since you're not actually sure if it's true.

Thrive on the fact Steve from accounts was seen coming out of the local Italian restaurant at lunchtime holding hands with Susan from marketing – well that was what Sharon said. Feel free to make a few choice alterations. For example, wouldn't the story be better if the restaurant became a local motel? Of course it would.

It will brighten up your day, keep you occupied and stop you getting bored when work levels are low. In addition you can also feel important until Steve finds out you have been talking about him and confronts you in the staff canteen. If your Steve is as big as our Steve, then you're in trouble.

Lies, rumours and stories of a malicious nature are the key to conflict, lack of trust, a slap and if you're lucky, a black eye. You must become a Mecca for the tittle-tattle of other gossips (who you'll note are usually the people who are going nowhere fast in your organisation). The simple rule is never say something to someone's face when you can say it behind their back.

There's plenty of fodder for you as well. Research has shown that seven out of ten UK employees admit to having had a fling with a colleague. Two-thirds of HR professionals said office affairs impacted negatively on productivity.

So by playing the percentages you can pick anyone in the office and they're more than likely to have a bout of stationery cupboard tomfoolery with someone around you at some point. It's a just a question of picking the other half of the offending party. We find the easiest way of doing this is to simply spin around three times and pick the first person you look at.

They say there is truth in every rumour – with your help we can make sure this simply isn't the case

You see, people love gossip but there's no way you're going to be taken seriously in the long run if gossip is how you choose to disseminate any information you think you have.

The damage you can do with a good bout of gossip is limitless. Take the example of Achal Singh, who was a librarian from Morena in India. Having worked there as a temporary worker for 12 years he demanded to be made a full-time member of staff. The rumour went around that bosses thought he was not of the right caste and thus would not make him full time. This led to poor Achal deciding there was only one thing for it – he vowed to wear nothing but his underwear and a single slipper to work until such time as he became a permanent employee.

"I will not wear clothes until I get justice," he was reported to have said.

SUCCESS WARNING!
Rise above the gossip. If you haven't got anything positive and constructive to say about anyone do not say anything. Take joy and happiness from people's successes and not their misery or failure.

Telling it like it is

At every given opportunity tell people what you dislike. Tell the smokers that you hate them smoking and that smoking breaks should be banned. Better still walk up close to them and start sniffing at their clothes.

Tell the drinkers that you don't like people who drink; tell new mothers that there's nothing wrong with child labour and tell the animal lovers that you are instigating Bear Baiting Thursday in the office.

> *"I am always doing what I cannot do in order that I may learn how to do it"*
> Pablo Picasso – *artist*

In short, vent your opinions without a care in the world. Whatever you do, don't take a moment to think whether or not what you are about to say is appropriate.

Successful people know when to speak and when to listen placidly, even in circumstances that they might find repugnant. This gives them time to evaluate and analyse said situation and decide how it might be turned to their advantage. There is almost always a silver lining if you look hard enough.

Might we recommend the fine art of 'blurting' to combat this restraint that we associate with successes? This means whenever something is done that you don't like, your brain immediately calls up your mouth and politely requests that you make a bizarre outburst that sounds like a startled horse. This should then be followed by an attack on someone's beliefs, actions or even characteristics that is as personal as you can make it.

If people complain that you are being invasive then remind them they are at work and that the company has kindly bestowed 104 days a year on staff when they can take time for personal matters – these special days are called Saturday and Sunday.

Once again we can head to South America for inspiration. Take Brazilian university professor Dias Aghiarian who called one of his students a 'fatty'. Aghiarian said that she was a 'fatty' who would get even fatter if she didn't change her diet when the pupil in question left a lecture to go to the toilet. This insensitive outburst earned him a £600 fine after she left her tape recorded running so as to not miss any of the lecture. When she played it back his ill-judged comments were clearly audible.

> *"Look at every obstacle as an opportunity"*
> Dr Wayne Dyer – motivational guru

We at the College of Failure encourage such traits in all our professors too. In fact, after years of practice, we can say with fair certainty we don't like you, although we're not sure quite why yet. If you have a moment to meet up so we can resolve this issue then that would be most kind.

SUCCESS WARNING!

Successful people know when to speak and when to listen placidly, even in circumstances that they might find nauseating. This gives them time to evaluate and analyse said situation and decide how it might be turned to their advantage. They believe there is almost always a silver lining if you look hard enough – even if the silver lining is a way to change their behaviour or learn from a good example of what not to do.

Practice makes perfect

If you happen to be talented at something make sure you believe that you never have to practice. Practice does indeed make perfect and that's something we want to avoid at all costs.

Forget about building on your natural strengths and never put in the time and effort to hone your skills. This way you'll avoid any opportunity to go from good performance to exceptional performance.

Avoid looking for ways to build on your skills – whether this be in a practical sense or through any kind of training. That way lies success! We can't stress enough that you should let any innate promise you may have go to waste. It is your God-given right to squander your God-given talents.

So laugh in the face of new experiences! Throw mud at anyone who dares offer you instruction of any sort. Chase them down the street if necessary so they never darken your door again.

Take this example of skulduggery from Pieterburen, near Groningen in Holland, where a man came back to his flat to find a strange car parked in his driveway. In the back seat of the car he found a couple of children. He asked them what they were doing there. They happily responded that their mummy and daddy were inside the house robbing him. Now these people had managed to get past the burglar alarm and into the house without anyone noticing so clearly they had a certain amount of aptitude in this field. However, they clearly hadn't taken any time to hone their talent and notice that leaving their children outside with clear instructions about what they were doing might be detrimental to their enterprise.

That's just the kind of pig-headed waste of talent that we're trying to foster. Incidentally the whole family escaped with nothing.

SUCCESS WARNING!
Successful people build on their strengths and then put immense amounts of effort in to hone their skills to reach an exceptional level of performance. Your talents exist in a unique combination and will drive you to success if you nurture and develop them.

Feeding yourself backwards

Listen and lap up positive feedback. No, we haven't gone stir-fry crazy, just hear us out. Yes, we admit a successful person will pay attention to when he or she gets positive feedback as they get the chance to realise what went right and why. You, however, need to combine it with a wilful disregard of any negative or developmental feedback you might attract. Be rude to the person who is giving it to you and start an argument if you feel the urge.

Accepting or, God forbid, asking for feedback when things go wrong is a very important route to success. That way you learn just why things went the way they did and you will find that people display a certain amount of respect at your willingness to learn from your mistakes.

As you've no doubt picked up, we are not big fans of such an approach.

> *"I am never a failure until I begin blaming others"*
> Anonymous

As we have said previously the only reason you should pay any attention to negative feedback is so you can recognise your best mistakes when you make them again.

Take this guy for example who got angry at the feedback he got from a company after not getting a job. He refused to accept the feedback they had given him, and like a man after our own heart wrote the following letter to the company:

> *I have received your letter informing me of your decision. I would have thought that there would have been more feedback with this decision than the scant information given.*
>
> *Your company, having first asked me to attend an interview and second making their decision, must now pay me for my inconvenience, including travel and my time taken out to be interviewed.*
>
> *Therefore, there is an outstanding account for 160 miles travel @ 0.42p/miles = £67.00 + 3hrs @ £21/hr = £63.00 making a total outstanding amount of £128.00.*
>
> *I will expect a cheque to be forwarded to me within the next seven days.*
>
> *Thanking you in advance for the assistance you have given me.*
>
> *Chris X*

Not only did he not like the feedback (the person who provided this letter assures proper feedback was given) but he ignored it and made financial demands in return. This guy is a genius. To our knowledge the company refused to pay up.

So your goal here is a hefty dose of self-denial. Lap up positive feedback and then sit back and wallow in your own genius. There is no more room for improvement – you are clearly close to perfection. Anyone offering constructive feedback on why things went wrong should be shunned. It goes without saying that you should be sure never to ask for feedback voluntarily; it will only ever lead to improvement and development. That gives us goose bumps and light nausea just thinking about it.

If you refuse to change and keep everything exactly as it is, the best you can hope for is stagnation and all the unpleasant smells that come with it. In the interest of knowing your enemy have a look at the questions posed by business specialist Jack Cranfield:

- What's changing in my life that I'm currently resisting?
- Why am I resisting that change?
- What am I afraid of with respect to this change?
- What am I afraid might happen to me?
- What's the payoff for my keeping things the way they are?
- What's the cost I'm paying for keeping things the way there are?
- What benefits might there be in this change?
- What would I have to do to cooperate with this change?
- What's the next step I could take to cooperate with this change?
- When will I take it?

If you can answer these and act upon them then nothing will be able to stop you and your success. Fortunately, we've already covered the notion of asking questions and thus you have hopefully already skipped straight ahead.

"There is the greatest benefit in making a few failures early in life"

Thomas H Huxley – anatomist

SUCCESS WARNING!

A successful person will pay attention when he or she gets positive feedback as they get the chance to realise what went right and why.

However, asking for feedback when things go wrong is a very important route to success. You will find that people display respect at your willingness to learn from your mistakes. Successful folk are constantly looking for improvements and developments, evaluating the benefits and costs of change and as appropriate implementing change for the better. However, be wary to avoid change for change's sake.

Letting it all hang out

We have seen that a tip top short cut to failure is to always consider yourself to be right. An off-shoot of this is the active desire to prove others wrong. This is a great way to channel your angst and general bitterness.

While you could be pushing on in whatever it is you're up to and forging your own success, we recommend you bog yourself down in a mire of distrust and jealousy.

The successful types out there have an annoying habit of actively proving themselves better than the opposition rather than trying to do others down. There is nothing better guaranteed to outgratiate (we imagine that is the opposite of ingratiate) you with others than pointing out their weaknesses. People revel in the company of those they feel safe and relaxed around. Round you they ought to feel uneasy and should be steeling themselves for their next humiliation.

Some people might work their anger or jealousy out in the gym, others through a swift jog. You should take it out on your colleagues. A prime example of how anger can be constructively managed is that of 'damage therapy', where Spaniards in the town of Soria offer you the chance to smash things up after work to release your tension. The enterprising chaps in charge have hired out a scrap yard where stressed out execs can go and pick up a sledge hammer and beat the living hell out of cars, computers, TVs or what ever floats their angst-ridden boat. One guy commented after a session that "I come after a bad day at work – I take a mobile phone, put it on the ground and smash it to bits with a single thump. You cannot imagine how satisfying that is." If you, on the other hand, have an issue with someone, you need to delve into their affairs and try to do them a mischief as if your life depended on it.

There's nothing like an embittered and insecure person round the office to drive everyone else to distraction. Aim to drain every last bit of creativity and originality from your environment.

You should be a failure blood hound, sniffing out all the weaknesses around you and exposing them for all to see. Now go get 'em Fido!

SUCCESS WARNING!

Focus on your own strengths to get yourself ahead – don't spend your time doing others down. This will slow your own progress and will inevitably come back to bite you as your victims look for chances of revenge. Rise above petty jealousy; if you make others feel secure in your presence they will buy into what you are doing. Do this and you will never be lonely and you will go far.

> *"If you want to increase your success rate, double your failure rate"*
>
> Thomas Watson snr – *IBM founder*

Making a positive into a negative

If you are not too busy focusing on highlighting the shortcomings of others and bathing yourself in their inadequacy, it's worth noting that you can do yourself equal amounts of damage by focusing on your own shortcomings. A successful person will give their failings due note so that they can learn from them and improve, but they will not dwell on them.

We have noted before that you can look back on your old mistakes and – more often than not – laugh at them. This lets people realise that nothing is 'the end of the world'. As a student of failure you need to believe that every mistake you make is a personal cataclysm that brings into question the whole space-time continuum, let alone just your world.

We imagine that there are plenty of successes in your life; we merely ask that you ignore these and instead think about the things you most fear and the things you don't want.

Clever brain scientists have shown that the brain doesn't take negatives. So if we said to you: "Don't think of a pink elephant", the first thing you will think of is a pink elephant. See? And you're not even drunk. (Or maybe you are; it's really none of our business.)

So it follows that if you focus continually on all the things that you don't – or shouldn't – want, then that's what you'll tend to end up with.

Do you speak to yourself? Don't worry; you're not completely do-lally. In fact we all speak to ourselves via that little voice in our head. Therefore, the more negative things you say to yourself the more you are increasing your chances of failure. One handy tip: if anyone makes mention of your regular habit of listening to the mutterings in your head, you can be sure to scare them by saying: "You're just jealous the voices only talk to me."

On the other hand, those who always focus on their goals and their positive experiences are more than likely to find success flopping into their lap in a rather helpful manner. Their internal voices also tend to be a little friendlier.

Think about all the things that put you in a really bad mood and then do nothing about it. Just go on the rollercoaster ride of negative emotions and let it give you something to moan about.

These considerations extend into thinking before you act. Don't think: react. Never take time to stop and think and decide on your actions, mood or response. Just be like one of Pavlov's dogs in his experiments, which would drool involuntarily when presented with food. (We have the same problems with pavlova puddings but that is a story for another time.)

"You may not realise it, but a kick in the teeth may be the best thing in the world for you"
Walt Disney –
film maker

Successful people take a moment – and it only needs to be a moment – to evaluate the situation and avoid putting their foot in their mouth. As a student of failure you should only take your foot out of your mouth long enough to replace it with your other one.

SUCCESS WARNING!

If you think positive then positive things are much more likely to come your way. If your outlook is bright, you will feel able to succeed in what you are doing and take on ever greater challenges. If you concentrate on your failings, it will drag you and your career down.

Coaching Yourself

Reflect on the lessons learned from Intermediate Level Failure and fill in the blanks:

Goals
1 ....
2 ....
3 ....

Personal strengths
1 ....
2 ....
3 ....

Immediate challenges/blocks/problems
1 ....
2 ....
3 ....

Development of skills
1 ....
2 ....
3 ....

Achievements
1 ....
2 ....
3 ....

Goals – Make sure your goals are positive and are about the things you want in your life. These can be some of the failure points you want to stop or some of the success points you want to continue or start.

Personal strengths – Look for your strengths, these can include anything from behaviours, skills, values and attitudes.

Immediate challenges/blocks/problems – List here negative things that directly affect you.

Development of skills – The development of skills listed here should be relevant to the goals set and the ones you are looking to develop to achieve your success.

Achievements – List achievements that you are proud of.

Section the Third

Advanced Failure – Getting Into and Bringing Down the Organisation

Congratulations you are now playing with the Big Boys and Girls of failure. We're into realms of unparalleled damage and destruction. Here we learn just what you can do to damage yourself, your team and your whole business.

It's lonely at the top

One of the things that companies consistently fail to notice is that the skills that got an individual to the top are not necessarily the ones they need when they get there.

The book *Writers on Leadership* by John van Maurik highlights the clever chaps at The Centre for Creative Leadership (CCL) at Greensboro, North Carolina, USA who found that a successful executive would possess some of the following seven characteristics:

1   Outstanding track record – identified early as having high potential and having a string of successes.
2   Outgoing, well-liked, charming.
3   Technically brilliant.
4   Loyal and helpful to management, willing to make sacrifices.
5   Ambitious and managed career well.
6   Moved up during reorganisation or merger.
7   Excellent at motivating or directing subordinates.

Then in research after our own hearts, they studied what facts caused promising careers to derail. There were a number of danger periods summarised as:

- they lost a boss who had shielded them or covered for them in some way;
- they entered a new job for which they were not fully prepared and this was usually coupled with having a new boss whose style was different;
- they left behind them a number of little problems or 'bruised people' whom they had handled poorly or failed to handle at all;
- they were promoted in some way during a shake-up of the organisation and their behaviour was not examined for some time after the promotion;
- they entered a level of seniority where getting on with other people under highly stressful conditions became extremely important.

All these factors caused the executive's flaws to show up. When they looked at various careers they found that only two of these factors need to be there to cause a career to go off the rails. Nice and easy.

Interestingly enough these flaws emerged from strengths that had played a part their rise and now either were inappropriate or were being relied on too much. These included:

1. Insensitivity to others, an abrasive, bullying style, extreme impatience and disregard for the feelings or priorities of others.
2. Being cold, aloof, arrogant.
3. Betrayal of trust – (not about basic honesty but rather "one-upping" others or failing to follow through on promises).
4. Over-managing – failing to delegate or build a team
5. Being over-ambitious – thinking of next job, playing politics
6. Failing to staff effectively – selecting poor people or those in their own image.
7. An inability to think strategically – over-attention to detail.
8. An inability to adapt to a boss with a different style.
9. Over-dependence on an advocate or mentor.
10. Pushing themselves too hard.

Just to cheer up would-be or bone fide executives out there, the number of forced resignations of CEOs in the UK has risen from 1% of total terminations to 5% since 1995. Just goes to show once you're at the top everything won't automatically smell of roses.

SUCCESS WARNING!
A different set of skills is needed for those who make it to the top. Executive coaches are more in evidence than ever as companies wake up to this fact. Just because you were good at one level doesn't automatically mean you'll be good when given a different set of roles and responsibilities. Many people fail because they made this presumption.

Thanks for the memories
Right, if we're going to take on the whole organisation you're going to have the mental agility to do so. So let's look at how your memory works so you can either build it up to remember past failures or so

you can choose to live in blissful ignorance of days gone by. How does the World Memory champion remember 520 playing cards in random order, when asked to recall them having studied them only for 20 minutes? How do they teach people with poor memories how to remember 40 random words in order in only 15 minutes on TV entertainment shows?

The brain records things in three ways. These are:

1 *The Replacement Technique*: where you have already learned something, but got it wrong. Think of things you get wrong time and again – for example spelling a word. This is the most difficult method of learning since you've already fixed it firmly in your head.

2 *Repetition*: where we tell ourselves something time and again until it sticks in your noggin. This is hard work and not as successful as you'd like.

3 *Association*: the best way, where we learn by linking one thing to another. Memories work in chains and are linked to things that come before and after them. To illustrate this take the list of things you have to buy today. Say you need: bacon, a table, toilet rolls, a dog, newspaper, a semi-detached house, new Wellington boots, a birthday card for the mother-in-law etc. etc. We've tried to choose really obscure things to make the point about how easy this is. Try just looking at this list and repeating the words to yourself without looking. It's not all that easy.

Next, tell yourself a story involving all these things. The story needs to be multi-sensory. Picture the story in your mind: see what you would see, hear what you would hear and feel what you would feel.

For example:

You walk into your kitchen and smell freshly cooked **bacon**, *you turn round and see it lying on the big round* **table**, *a beige puppy* **dog** *walks in carrying* **toilet rolls** *in its mouth but drops them and runs off with today's* **newspaper** *which has a picture of you on the front. You go to follow it but have to put on your bright red* **Wellington boots** *first and follow it towards a very small wooden*

semi-detached house. *You knock on the door and it is opened by your furious* **mother-in-law** *who demands to know why you forgot her* **birthday card.** *You rush off to buy a card...*

If you repeat it once or twice then all the things should be locked away to be recalled when you get to the shops. This technique of memory through association works for everything.

The act of remembering things is much easier if there is something to link it to, but it doesn't have to work in chains as above. Visual associations by themselves work a treat. This is why people learn language much quicker in foreign countries. They see something like a delicatessen and remember what it was called last time. This is much easier than staring at a book and saying the word over and over again.

The process is enhanced by all sorts of stimuli – sounds, smells, sights, emotions and so on. This is why emotional events tend to be ones where you say "I remember it like it was yesterday..."

Even the most abstract things can be remembered if you use association. Take surnames of people, their jobs and where they work. For example, one of your Professors is Mr Millar who is (at the time of writing) a deputy news editor. If you'd just met briefly with the aforementioned Mr Millar – say in a busy room where you're networking – you might easily forget names, jobs etc. But what if you looked at him (and my, isn't he handsome?) and imagined a man with flour on his hands outside a windmill and wearing a deputy sheriff's badge? That makes things much easier.

If you just want to be able to put a name to a face then when you first meet someone look for a characteristic – a huge nose for example – that stands out as this will act as a simple form of association. If they look like someone famous, that works too.

As you will have seen throughout this book we love working with animals. With this thought in mind we challenge you to test out the memory technique. The next four people you meet for the first time, decide which one of the following types they are. Picture them as one of these dogs and then remember their name.

The sheepdog – which rounds up everybody and makes sure they're all o.k.

The springer spaniel – playful but perhaps not the most intelligent

The labrador – friendly, solid & dependable

The terrier – won't let go until they're done

The bulldog – the powerful top dog that scares the others into doing what they wish

Remember, it's a dog meet dog world out there!

SUCCESS WARNING!

Memory works best by association and just trying to learn something in isolation is really difficult. Make use of all sorts of stimuli as well as the chain technique above if you quickly need to learn a set of facts or imprint any sort of memory upon your brain. To some people names are important, for example as a leader if you know the names of your staff and customers it shows they are important to you.

Mr Demotivator

If you set out to motivate people the easiest way to fail is to assume that what is important to you and what motivates you is what motivates those in your care.

What you know, even if others don't, is that they are just the same as you. They all have the same values, standards, ethics, needs, working style, personality traits and drivers as you. On the other hand, successful folk will insist 'each to their own' and analyse and treat people accordingly.

Might we suggest that you approach things in a similar way to Mayor Hugo Uzair of 9 de Julio – an Argentine town named after the country's Independence Day. He forced all public sector workers (about 70% of the town's workforce) to attend his birthday party – and they even had to pay for the privilege.

He was so sure that everyone wanted to share his joy that on arrival at the party, they had to sign a book to show they attended. If staff protested that they couldn't afford to go, the Mayor's office kindly said it would deduct the price from their wages, thus negating the need for any small change.

The sheer pigheadedness – or genius if you will – of this plan was summed up by the mayor's mother Fatima Uzair, who is an MP for the town. "People love my Huguito [Little Hugo]," she said. One has to wonder whether or not Mrs Uzair has touched base with reality recently.

The simple fact is that people live their lives by different, rules, standards and guidelines. Successful people need to take huge amounts of time understanding each person individually. This is great news for you as it leaves plenty of time to sit in your office listening to music. Again let us cast an eye across to Huguito who is probably bopping along to the strains of 'It's my party and you'll cry if I want you to'.

SUCCESS WARNING!

Successful folk realise that if they are going to motivate others the best way is to analyse and treat individuals as that: individuals. People have different values, standards, and needs. They will display flexibility and adaptability in the way they deal with people and this will enable them to hit the buttons that motivate and inspire others. At the end of the day the only person who can truly motivate a person is themselves. As a leader all you can do is create an environment where this can happen.

The wrong words at the wrong time

You will doubtless have heard the phrase 'think before you speak' many times. The reason you have heard it so many times (directed at you or not) is because people have an alarming, yet reassuring propensity to babble the first thoughts that pop into their teeny tiny brains.

This is of course to be encouraged. For example, when they train company spokespeople to talk to the media, more often than not a spokesperson will be advised to stick to one sentence or one point for each answer. This means you are succinct, to the point and look terribly clever.

It's quite amazing how easy it is to offend if you take the time and effort. Opportunity is all around if you just act first and ask questions much, much later. Take the English National Opera, that hub of luvviedom. They banned new employees from using the word 'darling' when talking to colleagues.

> *"The best way out is always through"*
> Robert Frost –
> poet

An education document, which is fortunately succinct, prohibits: 'suggestive remarks or lewd conduct that denigrates or ridicules or is intimidatory or physically abusive of an employee because of sex...or insults which are gender related...The use of affectionate names such as 'darling' will also constitute sexual harassment'.

We're not sure if the word 'dahhhling!' counts or not but we're going to try it nonetheless.

SUCCESS WARNING!

There's nothing more likely to propel you on the road to success than well-ordered, rational or intuitive thought which in turn leads to a well-constructed and timely view or decision. Understand the norms of your environment. Make strategic decisions having looked at the situation from multiple views and perspectives. With a bit of practice you can avoid blurting out utter nonsense without too many problems.

The Ethical Dilemma

The simple answer to a moral dilemma is not to have one. Too often you see these Hollywood blockbuster films where the good guy wrestles with his conscience while you're shouting: "Take the money, you fool! Leave the damsel to her fate!" Evenings round the TV at the College of Failure are never sedate affairs, we can tell you.

The urge to do the right thing in favour of the thing that benefits you instead must be suppressed at all costs. Where ever possible ensure you are making a negative or damaging contribution in some way – be it to individuals, a team, the organisation, an industry or society.

The successful person understands that making the morally right decision will benefit them in the long run. It breeds all those despicable characteristics we are trying so hard to avoid, such as trustworthiness and companionship. If everyone took this approach the world would be a better place. Fortunately we are only concerned with one world and that's your world. We find it rather comforting living in our own little world – everyone knows us there.

Making ethically dubious decisions will catch up with you in the end. People always find there will be the consequences, recriminations and negative emotions that will return with a vengeance. We've already quoted Horace at you, but it's too good an opportunity to miss, so remember that "raro antecedentem scelestum deseruit pede poena claudo". Now you are a consummate Latin scholar we won't bother with the translation again.

If you find yourself in the happy position of being forced to choose between two evils, we recommend you pick the one you haven't tried before. Live by the sword and you will die by the sword.

In order to focus your mind when you are faced with crises, your first job is to seek to understand the ethics (morals) of the situation. Once you understand them you can then work outside them like the good little failure that you are. The next question is just what standards you choose to play by. We all have them, but they are very often not consciously known.

> *"Success is 99 percent failures"*
> Soichiro Honda – *manufacturer*

So write down the rules and standards the Successful You (or evil twin, if you will) would wish to live by.

Once you have done this, all you will need to do for failure is at every opportunity break them. A nice, easy lesson that one.

If positive action is not your style then you can always just turn a blind eye to the ethical misbehaviour of others. You might be a member of Greenpeace and spend your summers swinging from tree to tree with your favourite orang-utans, while your company devastates vast areas of rainforest. There's nothing quite like abandoning your morals to make you feel as low and dirty as a seagull in an oil slick.

This is especially true if the organisation is doing something illegal. If you're really lucky they'll ask you to get involved, whereupon you must jump at the chance. You can be sure that when they are rumbled you will be the scapegoat – the evil one who could and should have stopped things.

Roger Steare, ethics advisor at Getfeedback, the talent management consultancy, uses the 'R.I.G.H.T.' technique. This offers five rules to help you decide whether or not something you have seen or have been asked to do is on the level:

Rules: If what is going on breaks either company rules or the law then you should act.

Integrity: Are you sacrificing your personal values?

Good: Who will benefit from this and how? Is it just a couple miscreants rather than customers, shareholders or staff as it should be?

Harm: Who will suffer from this and how?

Truth: Do you find yourself telling porkies to stay out of trouble? If you were to wake up to find your company splashed across the newspapers could you say you personally were in the clear? Or is it time to get that one-way ticket to Barbados?

SUCCESS WARNING!

The successful person understands that making the morally right decision will benefit them in the long run. He or she knows the first job is to seek to understand the ethics (morals) of the situation and appreciated how they align with the rules and standards they wish to live by.

Never a kind word

You'd be astounded just how far you can go if you say your Ps and Qs and actually take time to thank those around you or congratulate them on a job well done. This is a lesson that is particularly applicable to those in positions of power. (We like you at the College as you can take us out to lunch on expenses.)

Here at the College of Failure there are no staff except the stoic pair of sherpas who are presently leading you up Mount Ne'erdowell. One of the main reasons for this is we practice what we preach and *never* listen out for others, compliment them or say "please" and "thank you".

Some people say 'you can't get the staff these days'; we can get them but we don't have a hope in hell of keeping hold of them.

It doesn't take much to recognise a person's effort or achievement. You don't need to pay them anything extra necessarily, you just need to say 'well done' and make it clear you have noted that achievement.

Very few people take the time to do this to their fellow (wo)man. If they do it tends to be done inconsistently which upsets everyone sooner or later.

Recognition is a primeval urge and, as always, we can prove it. A study by the Yerkes National Primate Research Centre in Atlanta in the US found that chimpanzees who were given different rewards having done the same tasks got rather angry at the injustice. In a move that will give trade unions hope for recruitment in about 2 million years time once evolution has got involved, one chimp downed tools after he was given a cucumber when his colleague was given a banana for completing the same task.

So you see if you play the recognition card properly, it will make a monkey out of us all. We came across the following comments which come from real performance appraisals. They are perfect for our needs and will be sure to demotivate others and make sure they have no interest in ensuring your success in return:

1. Since my last report, this employee has reached rock bottom and has started to dig
2. I would not allow this employee to breed
3. This associate is not so much of a has-been, but more a definitely won't be
4. This young lady has delusions of adequacy
5. Works well when under constant supervision and cornered like a rat in a trap
6. He sets low personal standards and then consistently fails to achieve them

> *"The things which hurt instruct"*
> Benjamin Franklin – *inventor*

SUCCESS WARNING!

You'd be astounded just how far you can go if you say your Ps and Qs and actually take time to thank those around you or congratulate them on a job well done. It takes very little time but will lift them and their performance. This can only help you; your team will perform better and the glory for their successes will reflect on you.

A quiet word in your ear...

At the other end of the scale from politeness and recognition is outright unpleasantness and hostility. Swearing and using inappropriate language is the key. The more people you can shock, offend and upset the better. Might we recommend the words ****, ******, ******* and ******** for starters? (When the audio version of this book becomes available there's going to be trouble!) Being patronizing and arrogant can only help increase the impact.

All this might sound obvious and – since most people are seeking success – something that they would naturally avoid. Then how come we find ourselves surrounded by surly, unpleasant folk day in and day out? And we wise folk at the College of Failure are willing to bet you've been that surly person yourself on occasion.

If you haven't been that unpleasant reprobate then you need to concentrate hard on this lesson. Put down your book and go to the window. Warm up by hurling insults at anything you see in front of you, whether it be the neighbours, someone parking or a passing cat – don't let anyone feel safe from the depths of your uncouth tirades.

If you keep it up, there is no doubt you'll be the most unpopular person around.

Take this example of several bouts of harassment that ended tears for a 42-year-old Polish lady. She was jailed for running around an Italian castle pretending to be a ghost. The owners complained to police after hearing creaking floor boards, strange disembodied footsteps and slamming doors. The police set up hi-tec equipment to work out what on earth (or not, as the case might be) was going on.

They captured her charging up and down the corridors doing her best to stop the owners keeping their spirits up. She claimed in court that the castle owners were treating her husband – an employee at the castle – badly. She didn't stand a ghost of a chance and got four months in jail for her efforts.

If this isn't enough for you, we can't help but share the following letter of resignation that a member of staff at a leading computer company left on her manager's desk, demonstrating just how being unpleasant can catch up with you...

Dear Mr ******,

As a graduate of an institute of higher education, I have a few very basic expectations. Chief among these is that my direct superiors have an intellect that ranges above the common ground squirrel. After your consistent and annoying harassment of my co-workers and me during the commission of our duties, I can only surmise that you are one of the few true genetic wastes of our time.

Asking me, a network administrator, to explain every little nuance of everything I do each time you happen to stroll into my office is not only a waste of time, but also a waste of precious oxygen. You will never understand computers. Something as incredibly simple as binary still gives you too many options. You will also never understand why people hate you, but I am going to try and explain it to you.

You walk around the building all day, shiftlessly looking for fault in others. You have a sharp dressed useless look about you that may have worked for your interview, but now that you actually have responsibility, you pawn it off on overworked staff, hoping their talent will cover for your glaring ineptitude. In a world of managerial evolution, you are the blue-green algae that everyone else eats and laughs at. Since this situation is unlikely to change without you getting a full frontal lobotomy reversal, I am forced to tender my resignation. However, I have a few parting thoughts.

1. When someone calls you in reference to employment, it is illegal for you to give me a bad reference. The most you can say to hurt me is "I prefer not to comment". I will have friends randomly call you over the next couple of years to keep you honest.

2. I have all the passwords to every account on the system and I know every password you have used for the last five years. If you decide to get cute, I am going to publish your "favourites list", which I conveniently saved when you made me "back up" your useless files. I do believe that terms like "Lolita" are not usually viewed favourably by the company.

3. When you borrowed the digital camera to "take pictures of your Mother's birthday", you neglected to mention that you were going to take pictures of yourself in the mirror nude. Then you forgot to erase them like the techno-moron you really are. Suffice it to say I have never seen such odd acts with a sauce bottle.

Thank you for your time, and I expect the reference on my desk by 8:00 am tomorrow. One word of this to anybody and all of your little twisted repugnant obsessions will be open to the public. Never f*** with your systems administrator.

Wishing you a grand and glorious day.

Need we say more?

SUCCESS WARNING!

Successful people will regulate their behaviour and language to ensure they do not offend. This does not mean they show weakness or fear – they merely persuade rather coerce. But never hold it all in – if you suppress your emotions it is a recipe for disaster as you become a human pressure cooker. Instead share them with a coach, confidant or friend.

We are now a part of the tribe

Research shows that over 75% of dismissals or resignations are because a person does not fit into the culture of the organisation and only 25% are because they can not do their job. We imagine you've heard it said time and again: 'a person leaves their manager, not their job'. Your manager will tend to engender the organisation and its values. If they don't then they'll be off too, sooner or later.

With this in mind it becomes clear that you, the student of failure, need to work hard to make sure you do everything you can to make sure you don't fit in with culture of your company.

Corporate culture is "the way things are done around here". Unless you are right at the very top of the tree then demanding the culture be changed will put you on the fast train to the job centre – first stop Redundantsville. Population: you.

Of course there is a school of thought that immersing yourself in the culture and letting it carry you along, never making a sound and never questioning actions nor debating the system is ideal for a good bout of failure. This is indeed true and we have covered this in the highly informative section entitled *being a shrinking violet*.

What we are talking about here is differentiating between:

1. doing nothing and sinking to the bottom (only dead fish go with the flow after all)
2. joining in with the culture but aiming to constructively change it where necessary (very dangerous for the student of failure) and
3. facing it front on with an attitude that is so bad the plants wilt when you go by.

Let's look at the third option – outright hostility to the Establishment. The successful person will look around and analyse the environment they are in and will quickly establish what it takes to get ahead within that setting. This does not mean he or she has to bow to bad practice, merely offer alternative methods in a constructive way as in option two above. This usually entails putting your case across by explaining patiently why you favour doing something in a different manner.

Patience is a virtue for the successful person as people tend to fear and oppose change. To succeed you need to give change time to settle in. It's a case of baby steps.

> *"More people fail through lack of purpose than lack of talent"*
> Billy Sunday – evangelist

As long as the approach is constructive and not the rantings of a crazed loon, then all will be well. This is why corporate mergers and acquisitions fail so often. One company joins with another but the staff have entirely different ways of working and expectations. So they end up banging heads, doing less work and sooner of later the stock price starts to fall. We love mergers and acquisitions here at the College as it offers the potential for failure on a truly global scale and all because no one took the time to have a gander at the corporate culture.

A rather good analogy is a famous experiment carried out with fleas. If you put fleas into a glass jar and then put a glass lid onto the jar. The fleas will all bounce up and down hitting their head on the lid and then the bottom of the jar and back up again. They will continue to do this until doomsday.

If you were to take the glass lid off after a couple of hours you would find that the fleas continue to jump to exactly the same height as where the lid was, even though it has been removed. After another couple of hours one flea will probably jump higher by mistake and all of a sudden all his or her compatriots will do the same.

The same principle can be applied to business. One person – who has assessed the environment well – will challenge the status quo and suddenly everyone will join in. This is how progress happens. You could be that flea.

By this stage you should have realised what to do. Instead of taking the well-planned leap of our aforementioned flea, it's time for a culture clash of seismic proportions. It's time to grind against your company's customs in a manner that will register on the Richter scale.

If your company is keen on hierarchy then cut across it all and tell the CEO what you think. Feel free to address him or her by their first name as well. If collective decision making is the done thing then ignore it and pronounce your own verdict. If anyone says anything, make overtones about them being Commies and start a witch hunt under the guise of protecting Western democracy.

The coup de grace, we find, is to harp on about how great it was at your last firm and how you did things there. People *really* hate that.

Might we also return you to our dressing room of failure, so ably illustrated in *The apparel oft proclaims the man*. If suits are worn at work, we recommend t-shirts. If shiny shoes are the thing, then flip and flop your way into work in your favourite beach shoes.

The chances are that if your company has evolved a certain culture then that's what works in the circumstances. If this is not the case and things need to change, it needs to be done step by step. If the business is so resistant to change then it's doomed because competitors won't hang around to wait.

With that in mind, let your mind run riot. The wilder and more radical changes you can envision and the brashness with which you engender your efforts can only hasten your own demise.

A particular hero of ours in this field is Dean Wooten, who at the time of writing was a venerable 65-year-old from Des Moines, Iowa. Dean was employed as a greeter at Wal-Mart and had seven years of service under his belt.

In a moment of madness (we like to call it 'clarity') he decided he should start greeting shoppers to the store (to use the American parlance) holding a computer-generated picture of himself naked except for a sack covering his Mid West area, if you catch our drift.

Dean was telling shoppers that Wal-Mart was cutting back on expenditure and this would be his new uniform.

> *"When you fall, don't get up empty handed"*
> Unknown

Wooten was kindly asked to desist in this bare-faced cheek, but managers soon heard tell that he was showing his wares off again. So they fired him. The matter came to court and Dean said the whole thing was a joke and he didn't mean to bring the company into disrepute. Law Judge, Susan Brightman, did not share his optimism and ruled: "A reasonable person would know the act of showing a naked body wearing a Wal-Mart sack would not be good for business."

So at the end of the day, for all his efforts, Dean faced the ultimate irony: he got the sack.

SUCCESS WARNING!

The successful person will look around and analyse the environment they are in and will quickly establish what it takes to get ahead within that setting. They will invest time to understand the organisational style, values, beliefs, rituals and behavioural norms. This does not mean he or she has to bow to bad practice, merely offer alternative methods in a constructive way. This usually entails putting your case across by explaining patiently why you favour doing something in a different way.

Judging a book by its cover

Once upon a time, in a land far, far away, there existed companies that operated in very set structures where social and business hierarchies dictated exactly who you were and what you did. Job titles said it all and Heaven forefend people thought or acted outside these boundaries. In the modern age this simply isn't the case anymore.

There will be plenty of people around you who will appear to be in straight forward roles with well-defined parameters. In your infinite wisdom, you need to work on the assumption that a person's power in the organisation is limited to the position the individual holds.

The fact the secretary Belinda has the ear of the CEO because she has worked with him or her for the last 20 years is totally irrelevant. Ignore Belinda, she is clearly beneath you – a mere secretary? Pah! The fact that this secretary knows all the information about the organisation can be ignored out of hand.

The fact that Barney from IT plays golf with the MD does not matter either, he can go swing for all you care. What matters is the rigid structure that the hierarchy of the organisation should create.

The informal networks, relationships and history are where a lot of power lies in any organisation. Analysing the relationships people have beyond their job titles is a powerful way of working out just who will be important in the race for success. Luckily this is a race where you have already dropped the baton and have retired having implicated yourself in a doping scandal.

The only thing you have to remember here is to ignore the subtleties of office relationships – strive to perpetuate the myth of

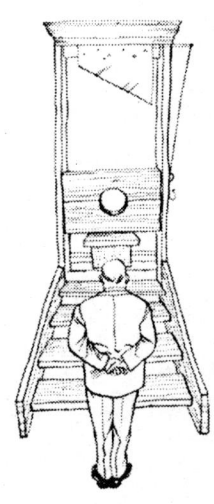

rigid office pecking order like the office-based aristocrat you are. In this modern day and age your behaviour can only lead you one place – the guillotine.

It's also worth believing that everyone is working towards the company agenda and no one has their own personal agendas. If you were to take a moment to work out who wants what in the office, it would put you in very good stead and enable you to react accordingly. Of course, as a student of failure you will be fresh out of such available moments.

SUCCESS WARNING!

The informal networks, relationships and history are where a lot of power lies in any organisation. Analysing the relationships people have beyond their job titles, as

well as their personal agendas, is a powerful way of working out just who will be important to you as you strive for success and influence.

Please lie down on the couch...

If a desperate lack of subtlety is not your style then might we recommend you adopt the psychiatrist approach? Wrap your big loving arms around the company and everyone therein. Don't let go until you've suffocated the lot of them with your boundless affection.

Become so sensitive to the problems of others that nuns shy away from you in disgust. Impose yourself on people and their private torments like an American talk show host. (If you choose to walk around chanting your own name after you've successfully invaded the privacy of yet another colleague, then all the better.)

> *"Failure – the man who can tell others what to do and how to do it, but never does it himself"*
>
> Unknown

Use dulcet and patronising tones that imply weakness in others. Ask them awkward questions about their mothers – that's what the staple approach of all other psychiatrists seems to be. We'll even offer you a natty plaque that you can hang on the wall to officially announce your doctorate in Over-eager Intrusion.

It's important to make sure you go too far. People appreciate it when you acknowledge they might have a problem and they tend to like it when you offer your help. It makes them feel loved. What they don't like is becoming your next pet project and being imposed on by someone who clearly thinks they are a higher being with a greater grasp on how to get on in life.

These overbearing people are the kind of folk who would be arrogant enough to sit down and write a book about how to get ahead. Outrageous behaviour.

Might we recommend these wise words of George Bernard Shaw in his masterpiece 'Man and Superman', which will go a long way to making people who already feel down, feel thoroughly inadequate:

"This is the true joy of life, the being used for a purpose recognised by yourself as a mighty one: the being a force of nature, instead of a feverish little clod of ailments and grievances complaining that the world will not devote itself to making you happy".

Under the guise of passing on a bit of your serenity you will annoy people with your intrusion and will make them question themselves even more as they try to work out whether or not you are just trying to help. By the time they have dwelled on this for a bit they will truly detest you.

Then you know that your work is done – give yourself a congratulatory hug. There's a lot of love here.

SUCCESS WARNING!

Successful people take a keen interest in other people and their lives. However, they set clear boundaries to ensure they do not violate or intrude into people's personal affairs.

Taking a view on an interview

Time to consider just how you could avoid getting that job you're after. If you are going for a new role forget who else is going for it and ignore the attributes, qualifications, experience and expertise needed for the role. You would be shocked and amazed at the proportion of people who turn up for an interview having not looked at the requirements of the job or having any inkling of what the company is about. Just taking these simple steps will automatically put you above the churning masses of people trying to get a new job.

If it is an internal interview, just tell the interview panel how great you are and that you deserve the job because you have been here the longest. Applying your own attributes to the requirements of the role is something you need not waste your time on as that's the way to succeed. Make sure your preparation is also a lonesome task as asking people for help is a sure-fire way of getting a broader and better-informed take on your talents and how they apply.

Having declared to your superiors the job should be yours due to some obscure right that you can't quite explain, proceed to bad mouth, back stab and tell lies about the others applying for the role.

The more unpleasant you can be the better. Research has shown that people who make recruiters laugh during the interview process are more likely to get the job and are more likely to earn more in subsequent performance bonuses.

The report found that the key doesn't lie in talking any more than anyone else but engaging others more successfully with the use of humour or even just a smile. Negative humour such as sarcasm doesn't do the job as well as positive banter. So be rude, crude and vile and they'll show you the door and then they'll bolt it behind you.

A lack of preparation is key as the phrase 'fore-warned is fore-armed' is very true. If you rehearse the things that you are likely to be asked then you will find you answer in a more succinct way in interviews and your brain will be clear to provide you with any extra points that spring to mind. Unless you are a truly exceptional individual you will not convince an interviewer if you make it up as you go along.

However, there is one form of preparation that we recommend at the College and that is adding a lie or two to your CV, just to spice it up. As simple as these lies may be they offer traps aplenty in an interview. The interviewer will almost certainly ask something about your trip to spread Christianity to small islands off the coast of Papua New Guinea, and as Sods Law dictates, he or she has probably visited there and will wish to discuss the natives' use of ceremonial penis gourds with you.

If you think you are unlikely to get caught out, here's a cautionary tale. A German chemistry student turned up for an interview with a professor of chemistry in Aachen.

> *"It is often failure who is the pioneer of new lands, new understandings and new forms of expression"*
>
> Eric Hoffer –
> *author*

Upon looking at the young man's CV, the interviewer grew suspicious and asked to see a notarised copy of the student's certificates of study. In a moment of genius, the student, who might just have been lying, grabbed his CV, ate it and sprinted from the office. This fully-paid up College of Failure member ensured his own demise by not eating the bit which had his address on it. He was charged with forgery by police.

> *"Failure, I never encountered it. All I ever met were temporary setbacks"*
> Dottie Walters –
> *speech guru*

Even the things you do actually do are good fodder for our purposes. Be wary what you list as your interests as eight out of ten recruiters say the things listed under hobbies and interests on a CV influence their recruitment decisions.

Too much detail can put them off immediately (so it goes without saying, the more you can tell them about your collection of human body parts the better). Successful types recommend that a CV should never be longer than two pages. Yours should be a thesis.

Highlighting weird or inappropriate interests are also unlikely to put you on the interview shortlists. Those who site 'drinking' as a chief recreation will be automatically discarded by one in four recruiters. This is why the cellars at the College of Failure are always well-stocked so students can have a drink or five before heading out to try and get a job.

SUCCESS WARNING!

Successful people do their preparation and research for whatever they do. There are few more important moments for this than on the occasion of an interview. They do not believe their own hype and are therefore more likely to put in an exceptional performance. The 80% preparation, 20% delivery rule applies. They know their next performance is the one that counts.

Having the vision to fail

The mind has difficulty differentiating between a visualisation and a reality. This is why top sports people like footballers David Beckham and Michael Owen spend time visualising taking kicks/penalties as a key part of their training. Before they touch a ball they are programmed to think it will go in.

Of course there isn't a 100% record but you imagine trying to do that in front of 60,000 people screaming obscenities at you. Better still come to the College and we'll do it for real, you lousy, cretinous… sorry, we got carried away.

Research has shown that this visualisation makes their bodies actually act out the action involuntarily. After clever boffins attached little electrodes to their bits, they found the same micro muscles move when the sportsmen imagine their actions as when they are actually doing them.

The message is that with the right mindset, you can do anything. Of course this takes failure to a whole new level – even the most successful person can plunge themselves into a pool of disappointment with a most satisfying belly-flop if they concentrate on the negative.

Therefore, use visualisation to picture things that you think are going to go wrong. As you prepare to make that presentation convince yourself that at any given point you are going to blurt out a rumour about the CEO being pregnant – even though you reckon the guy has just put on weight.

Look into our eyes…You know that you are going to fail. Yeeeeees…you know you can't get through the day…you know that your manager thinks you have done something wrong…let the paranoia spread…yeeees…listen to the voices…

"In great attempts, it is glorious even to fail"

Vince Lombardi – NFL *legend*

Look in a mirror and repeat this and any other worries or insecurities that are playing on your mind. You will programme yourself to fail.

To make the image even more powerful ensure that when you visualise a situation you see what you will see, feel what you will feel and notice what you would notice. This way you will be totally prepared for a bout of well-organised failure.

It has been proved that we automatically move in the direction of the things that dominate our thoughts and if we believe something to be true we see the world in that way. That's why you get the most unlikely folk succeeding. Take Casanova, for example. Hardly any woman in the known world was safe from his advances and yet he was reputed to have a face like a yak's bum. In his memoirs he numbers the amount of women who accepted his advances at 122, which included four people at once – one of whom was nun!

Visualisation can be a bit like wearing sunglasses. It offers you psychological protection and will automatically be reflected in the way you approach activities – even if it's just walking into a room.

Successful people will act as if they are already where they want to be. They will dress, talk, think and feel like the person they want to be when they have achieved a goal or outcome. This means that before they start out to tackle this goal they are well-prepared and have the mental equivalent of warm clothing and sturdy shoes for the journey. Their mothers would be proud.

SUCCESS WARNING!

Act as if you are already where you want to be. Dress like, talk like, think like and feel like the person you want to be when you have achieved your goal or outcome. This has an important impact in programming your brain to help you succeed. We automatically move in the direction of the things that dominate our thoughts and if we believe something to be true we see the world in that way. *Fake it until you make it.*

Feel the fear

If you're going to take on the whole organisation and ruin it then pay close attention to this lesson. One thing, possibly above all other, that marks a successful person from a failure is courage. One of the greatest lessons best-selling author Susan Jeffers highlights in her book 'Feel the fear and do it anyway' is that fears are natural and it is simply our body saying we are out of our comfort zone.

Our ancestors were hunted or were hunters and they often had real fears. The fresh meat counter at the local supermarket back then was stocked with woolly mammoth which you first had to stab to death.

The reality today is that if we do a presentation or have a key meeting or an interview no one is going to eat us; we are just out of our comfort zones. If you accept this as a fact of life then you can marshal your fear and use it to keep you sharp and ready.

Of course this is nonsense as far as we are concerned at the College.

Let us use those lovable rogues, the Ku Klux Klan, to illustrate just how Neanderthal things can still be.

> *"The greatest mistake in life is to be continually fearing you will make one"*
>
> Elbert Hubbard – *philosopher*

On the occasion in question a potential new member was tied to a tree and shot with paint pellets. This wasn't enough for one would-be recruitment consultant, Gregory Freeman, who fired his real gun into the air to add to the atmosphere. The bullet shot into the sky, before returning to earth through the head of Jeffrey Muir, another colleague in this Klan personnel department. It left Muir in a critical condition in hospital. We couldn't find out if the would-be member is still tied to the tree or not.

In this instance his fears were probably justified as he was surrounded by a group of crazed rednecks, one of whom was lying in a pool of blood. Even we at the College have to admit this kind of situation is rare in the civilised world – certainly anywhere that sells this book. Successful people take this on board and realise fears are just there to be overcome and no great harm will befall if they just give it a go.

So, dear reader, given an opportunity to move outside your comfort zone and achieve more, feel the fear and freeze. You'll find yourself so paralysed that you'll think you've been tied to a tree by a redneck with a shotgun. As soon as you've found your legs again, run away from what you are trying achieve as fast as your quaking legs will carry you.

There will be times when you overcome your fear and actually achieve something. Successful people return to the memories of these events to remind them how easy overcoming fears can be. Memories of these occasions can reassure you and spur you onto further success. For this reason these particular memories are the enemy of failure and must be shunned at all costs.

SUCCESS WARNING!
Successful people know the reality today is that if we do a presentation or have a key meeting or an interview no one is going to eat us; we are just out of our comfort zones. If you accept this as a fact of life then you can marshal your fear and use it to keep you sharp and ready.

Mind reading is not an open book

Here's a question for you: how often have you ever complained about the state of affairs at work or someone's behaviour without actually asking the relevant person why the situation exists, or offer your opinion about how things might be done better? Even worse, how many times have people afflicted you with complaints about something that is going wrong at their work? These folk are not only wasting their time, they are wasting yours, and thus must be congratulated by any self-respecting student of failure.

Those playing the success game know that no sympathy should be offered to people and

> *"If you are not failing every now and again it is a sign you're not doing anything innovative"*
> Woody Allen –
> *director*

their complaints until such time as they have actually tried to do something about them.

This is one of the great mistakes made at work – people presume that if you have a problem then others will know and understand what you are going through. Despite what you might read in astrology pages of the tabloids, no one can read your mind.

This is obviously your opportunity as a student of failure to give telepathy a damn good shot. Having explained that many of your colleagues live in blissful ignorance of your concerns, we recommend the hard-working student of failure should take to staring at them across the office really hard in the hope your worries will be transferred to their brains.

Now, stare harder, go red in the face and start to shake as if you are going to burst into flame. Will it make a positive difference? Almost certainly not – but then we're not in the business of getting things done are we? The bonus is people will think you're an utter nutter if you keep at it.

The reality is that the person or people that are causing your concerns probably have entirely different concerns about you and you, unless you are an absolute cad and are purposefully annoying them, will be unaware of them. Talking to people about what is bothering you or even just confusing you will probably ease your mind immediately.

You, on the other hand, need to convince yourself you live a weird wizarding world where people mysteriously know when you want something or want to learn something. If someone's achieved something, never ask them how they did it, they'll stroll by and read your mind at any minute, don't you worry.

If you get the urge to start bothering people and explaining just what you need to know then start rejecting yourself in advance. Believe people are going to say no. This takes us back to the whole issue of visualisation; take a moment to experience what it will be like to be rejected, look stupid, foolish or even needy when you ask for help.

SUCCESS WARNING!

Remember what we said earlier – if you have something to say, go to the person directly and deal with the issue rather than moaning to everyone else. The same principle extends to learning from others. If someone is really good at something, ask them how they do it. The amazing thing is that 99% of the time people will tell you the answer. They believe if one person can do it, so can others. The experts call this 'modelling excellence' – other people call it 'copying'.

Throw some darts and see how many stick

Often we have sat in meetings and listened to corporate people speaking as much jargon as they can and attempting to use long words or bizarre phrases. They think it is big and clever. It clearly is not...unless you're a student of the College.

The benefit of jargon is that you can force varying degrees of failure upon everyone in the room where you have opened your big mouth. Recent research of British office workers found that two-thirds of staff have colleagues who use unnecessary jargon to confuse people and attempt to make themselves look superior.

"Failure is only a temporary change in direction to set you straight for your next success"
Denis Waitley – productivity consultant

Many of those surveyed found it irritating and distracting and thought it made users sound pretentious and untrustworthy.

So on the one hand, you will come across as a complete prat and people will respect you less and less. On the other hand your pretentious ramblings will inevitably cause a range of emotions among those listening to you – from boredom to outright hostility. This will in turn make sure they can't pay attention to the job at hand and don't get anything done themselves. It's like synchronised failure.

If that's not enough for you, heaviest users of management jargon could face the police storming in at any moment declaring them a danger to society. Professor Robert Hare of the University of British Columbia did a study to root out 'corporate psychopaths' from organisations as they were the most likely to become violent or defraud the business.

Among things to look out for in this 'cut-throat' business world are people who can manipulate others without remorse and a veneer of charm which will get these corporate psychos on to the management fast track.

Other indicators that work is about to become sheer murder, include having an inflated self-image, unrealistic career goals and taking credit for the work of others. While this is all very interesting, we come to the nub of things: Prof Hare (not affiliated to the College of Failure by the way) concluded that one of the key indicators was 'using lots of management jargon to impress people'. If you do happen to be on the receiving end of these terrifying folk then it would be best to make what could be your last moments happy ones.

For those of you on the end of these pretentious rants we have included some buzzword bingo tables for you and your colleagues in the appendices. Not only will they take the edge of the fool who's demanding to know whether you're all singing from the same hymn sheet, but it will distract you completely and filter out any productive information that happens to come your way.

The idea is to just cross off the words as you say them or hear them said. The winner is the one who crosses them all off first. Feel free to create your own games; a few choice expressions are here to help get you started:

Think outside of the box, curve-ball, low-hanging fruit, e-tailing, talk off-line, blue-sky idea, win-win situation, think outside the box, holistic approach, level playing field, sanity check, put to bed, whole nine yards, helicopter view, gap analysis, touch base, rain check, sing from the same hymn sheet, finger in the air, get in bed with, big picture, benchmark, ball park, ticks in all the right boxes, strategic fit, bread and butter.

Please feel free to use these linguistic delights at your leisure.

SUCCESS WARNING!

No one appreciates management jargon. It is a far greater gift to be able to speak clearly and succinctly and people will recognise and appreciate this. It cannot be stressed enough that buzzwords will never, ever make you look or sound clever.

Speed is of the offence

The chaps from the success side of the fence always seem to have their radars out for opportunities. They pounce on them as they arise like steroid-fuelled panthers. Successful people tend to work faster than the average man in the street and they always seem to achieve things faster.

In fact we live in a world where people are constantly striving for quicker and faster results. Is this because they attempt to do everything at light speed? No. The key to their success is they are remarkably well-organised and simply slot each new challenge into their schedule as and when they come along. They don't get flustered, they don't get worried; they take one thing at a time.

You'd be surprised how easy this is. A mere list of things 'to do', put in order of preference will lift the weight of your many tasks off your shoulders with the strength of an Eastern European shot putter.

You, on the other hand, need to become a human tornado, rushing around scattering paper, people and the odd cow or two wherever you go. Be obsessed with saving time, count the amount of minutes each week you save and then do nothing with them. This will drive you mad.

All around us there are stimuli to help you be rushed off your feet. Isn't it odd that if someone asks you: "Are you keeping busy?" that it's socially unacceptable to say no?

FIVE MINUTE FAILURE

Allow speed to rule your thoughts and actions and be in a permanent state of agitation. This is easily achieved by never stopping to take a deep breath. Before you know it the world will climb on top of you and you'll feel like a rather pathetic version of Atlas. (For those of you who didn't pay attention at school – and well done by the way – he was the Greek God charged with carrying the world on his back. We want to know what on earth he was standing on.)

The modern world offers you opportunity after opportunity to do things at speed, which means you'll never have to sit back and appraise the situation if you don't want to.

Since you've got no time for anything (why are you reading this, damn it? There's no time!) we've taken a moment out of our ridiculously busy schedule to set out all the moments in your day that might be used to push the failure envelope:

Wake up in the middle of the night. Take stock of the impossibly large number of tasks that face you when the sun comes up. Put aside any thoughts of dealing with things when you actually can (i.e. when the rest of the world has woken up and joined in). Needless worrying about things you cannot change at that moment is one of our favourite failure methods. Don't eat a proper breakfast as you do not have time – just grab a breakfast bar on your way out. Starting the day without a decent meal is like running a car without petrol; it doesn't work too well and soon you'll start to smell.

Having not fuelled your metaphorical car, jump in your real one and drive to the train station as fast as the speed limit allows. Put your make-up on as you drive. If you are taking this seriously, the fact you may never worn make-up before won't be important as you'll be too busy to notice. Quickly: remember you need to ask your cleaner to get out your microwave meal for the evening.

In fact, don't call her as that will take time; text her on your mobile while eating the breakfast bar and driving with your feet.

You arrive at the station and run for the train. You grab a seat, pushing three women and a child out the way. Make that two children since one of the women was pregnant. Skim read the report you need for the meeting in fifteen minutes, then realise you do not need to be at the meeting as it is wasting time and cancel it. Spend the morning e-mailing everyone and then take a well-earned cup of coffee. If you have enough time to touch it before it gets cold then you're not busy enough.

Right about now a successful person would take 5 or 10 minutes to relax and take stock. They realise 5 minutes here and there really doesn't matter and you will more than make it up in extra productivity. No such respite for you. Back to your day... *Do not waste time making a new cup of coffee – that kettle takes too damn long to boil.*

By this time you've only reached mid-morning and we hope you've got the idea. This is only one morning but if you stick with it then you'll be too busy to see your children growing up and you certainly won't have the opportunity to make love any more as you'll be knackered.

> **"The most important of my discoveries has been suggested to me by my failures"**
> Sir Humphrey Davy – inventor

There is always enough time if you are prepared to be organised. When we are in control of our time we are at our happiest. This is why the self-employed tend to be happier than those employed by someone else. The self-employed tend to work longer hours but report they are happier with their work-life balance.

Ask yourself – does what you are doing matter to you? Does it make a difference and does it excite you? The reason time flies when we are having fun is because the body goes into what experts call a "flow state" where it is relaxed and focused. Ask yourself another question: "When does work not seem like work?" Successful people will use the answer to focus their career aspirations.

For the sake of scientific discussion, try taking five minutes when you feel stressed or flustered to get away from your desk and take stock. Take deep breaths and just let go of things for a moment. You'll find that it takes no time at all to relax and when you get back to your desk you'll be able to think more clearly.

There's a medical reason for this. When you get stressed the brain releases something called cortisol, which to cut a long story short, shuts down the part of your brain in charge of thinking creatively. This is based on a primal reaction that is supposed to leave you with the option of 'fight or flight'.

Your ability to think things through and indulge in some good quality analysis becomes mentally and physically impossible as your body prepares for 'fight or flight'. So at the end of the day it turns out the old adage rings true: all haste and no speed.

This is why we want you charging around like a drug-fuelled bull in a china shop every day of your life. Now go to it, there isn't a minute to waste...

"I cannot give you the formula for success, but I can give you the formula for failure – which is try to please everybody"

Herbert Bayard Swope – journalist

SUCCESS WARNING!

Rushing everywhere is not the key to getting more done. It has now been proved on a scientific level that more haste means less speed. Take a moment to stop and take stock of things whenever stress starts to set in. Just a few minutes to let your brain re-engage can make all the difference. There is always enough time – just make sure you're using it the way you want to and not how someone else is forcing you to.

Coaching Yourself

Reflect on the lessons learned from Advanced Level Failure and fill in the blanks:

Goals
1 ....
2 ....
3 ....

Personal strengths
1 ....
2 ....
3 ....

Immediate challenges/blocks/problems
1 ....
2 ....
3 ....

Development of skills
1 ....
2 ....
3 ....

Achievements
1 ....
2 ....
3 ....

Goals – Make sure your goals are positive and are about the things you want in your life. These can be some of the failure points you want to stop or some of the success points you want to continue or start.

Personal strengths – Look for your strengths, these can include anything from behaviours, skills, values and attitudes.

Immediate challenges/blocks/problems – List here negative things that directly affect you.

Development of skills – The development of skills listed here should be relevant to the goals set and the ones you are looking to develop to achieve your success.

Achievements – List achievements that you are proud of.

An Epilogue of Sorts

A final thought from our sponsors

In a moment of sincerity and seriousness (it won't happen again we promise) let's round up everything that you have learned on our journey together about what it takes to succeed.

Remember success and happiness should be one of a kind; they should go hand in hand. Failures are just milestones on the road to success and often take you closer to success. If they are not, you always have the option of getting off the road at the next exit and changing direction.

What ever you do remember this advice. Marilyn Monroe did when she was dropped by Twentieth Century Fox, because an executive thought she was unattractive; Laugh-o-Gram – Walt Disney's first cartoon production company – went bankrupt, and the Beatles were rejected by Decca Records, Philips, Columbia and HMV.

Then there was the school music teacher in Memphis, Tennessee who gave Elvis Aaron Presley a "C" grade and told him he could not sing. Failures really are milestones on the road to success.

Ask yourself are you happy? Motivated? Prospering and fulfilling your potential? If not, read this book again and this time reflect on how the lessons apply to the peculiarities of your life, making it real for you and making clear what action you need to take. It could change your life.

If you do nothing else remember the following lessons.

1   Attitude, resilience and optimism

Successful people have a positive mental attitude, they are resilient and bounce back quickly from setbacks. They are optimistic in their outlook – they expect the best and get it. As the famous saying goes "you get what you focus on".

In turn you will get what you deserve.

2   Visions, strengths, values and purpose

Successful people play to their strengths and natural abilities and in turn this means they end up doing what they enjoy. Be aware of your skills and weaknesses and surround yourself with people whose strengths will help bolster your weaknesses. Ensure everything you do is underpinned by your needs and values. This will give you a clear higher purpose for what you are doing.

3 Goals, practice and disciplined use of time

Successful people set goals which are milestones towards their visions and then practice, practice, practice their natural skills and abilities. This approach will speed you on to your ultimate goal.

4 Trust intuition, risk taking and action orientated

Successful people trust themselves and their intuition and take calculated risks. Put your decisions into action rather than being just talk. Walk the walk and remember to have the flexibility and adaptability to change along the way as and when appropriate.

5 Relationships, visibility, perceptions and personal brand

Relationships based on trust are key: you need people to help you achieve your visions. Take time to understand who you are and what you stand for. Ask yourself: "What is my unique brand?". Always remember this effort will be for nothing if you don't get visibility for your great work and manage the perceptions of others.

6 Leaders are learners who turn any situation to their advantage

Great leaders lead their own lives. They are constantly learning and they are often known for being lucky. The truth is they are lucky because they turn any situation to their advantage through the knowledge they have spent time accumulating.

7 Rounded whole people balance success and happiness

Work-life balance is not just a trendy management term. Successful people focus on aligning happiness and success and this means combining work and life, not making them opposites. You need to be a rounded person who is neither dominated by your job or by your life outside the office.

Finally – knowing this stuff is only the beginning, putting it into practise is the real test. This may sound like common sense but it is common practice that matters.

Having said that, for all you minimalists out there who believe reducing over 300 books to 7 points is still too much, the 3 point strategy for any success is:

- Have a compelling vision of what you want
- An action plan to achieve it
- The positive mindset to follow it through.

Once upon a time

One final test then, from your Professors.

Please take your time and spend around 3 minutes learning these words/phrases all 25 of them in order.

1. Optimistic
2. Bounced back
3. Vision
4. Higher Purpose
5. Leaders as learners
6. Perceptions
7. The Values
8. Visibility
9. Natural ability
10. Strengths
11. Trust
12. Goals
13. Adaptability
14. Flexibility
15. Work-Life balance
16. Happiness
17. Success
18. Relationships
19. Personal Brand
20. Visualised
21. Practiced
22. Intuition
23. Calculated risk
24. Rounded whole person
25. Lead their own life.

Without looking now write down all 25 in order – or as many as you can:

1
2
3
4
5
6
7
8
9
10
11
12
13
14
15
16
17
18
19
20
21
22
23
24
25

How many did you get?

Now spend 3 minutes reading the following story. As you read it, where ever possible visualise what you would see, hear what you would hear and feel what you would feel.

The story of Optimistic

Once there was a large bright orange rubber ball with a hole in the side called **Optimistic**. One day he was thrown at a wall and as always he **bounced back**. As he shook his head, his **vision** became clear and there in front of him was a sign post, pointing in the direction of the town in the hills called **Higher Purpose**. He set off on this journey with his book under his arm titled **Leaders as learners**. The first thing he came to was a bright pink sign for a theatre called **Perceptions** on it were pictures of a girl band with **The Values** written on their T-shirts. He walked in and it was totally dark and then the spot light came on him and he could see; he had **visibility**.

In his hand was a song sheet. Written on the top was the name of the tune called **Natural Ability**. He ran out of the stage door and bumped into two cats; a beautiful black cat called **Strengths** and a scruffy white one called **Trust**. Next he turned the corner and saw a number of football **goals** and beside them were two dogs. The first small, short and slightly overweight dog was called **Adaptability** and the tall slim dog was called **Flexibility**. They kicked him and he got stuck on top of the see saw. He looked down on one side and on the seat was written **Work-life balance** and the other seat **Happiness and Success**. Beside him was a red container with **Relationships** written on it, inside was a green tin of beans with the words **Personal Brand** on the front. Should he jump in? He had **visualised** this scene many times and had **practiced**, so he used his **intuition** and took a **calculated risk** and jumped. Inside was a mirror and as he looked in it, he saw a ball without the hole, a totally **rounded whole person** who **lead their own life**.

Now re-tell the story or re-write it (which ever you prefer) each time you come to one of the words write it down:

1

2

3

4

5

6
7
8
9
10
11
12
13
14
15
16
17
18
19
20
21
22
23
24
25

Now how many did you get?

If you remember the story of Optimistic you will be able to remember all the key learning points from this book. Now that is accelerated learning!!! And you thought you had a bad memory.

See Thanks for the Memories at the start of section three if you've forgotten what association chains are (which would be rather ironic!)

A final, final thought from our sponsors

The seven principles above make for an easy guide to getting ahead – and frankly do you have time for techniques that are so complicated they would make Stephen Hawking think twice before attempting them? Thought not.

These same principles only need to be adapted ever so slightly to be applied to a whole organisation. There is a lot of research around that suggests organisations mirror the personality of the ultimate leader of the organisation (especially in the early years of the organisation's formation) and the leader mirrors the organisation.

Therefore if you want to understand the organisation analyse the CEO and if you want to understand the CEO analyse the organisation and the challenges it faces. This works at a more micro level. Think of a team you work in, the challenges and problems the team faces, and how these relate to the leader and their personality.

So if you are that leader – CEO or team leader or whatever, it's worth baring in mind the following 7 principles for a successful organisation:

1. **Attitude, resilience and optimism** – successful organisations expect the best. They have to have a positive culture/attitude and need to be resilient and bounce back quickly from set backs. If a product or strategy is not working they need to be flexible to try something else and move quickly. They are optimistic in their outlook and believe in their products and services. They therefore expect the best and get it. This is done in an environment that encourages participation and doesn't put down people who have new and different ideas.

2. **Visions – strengths, skills, values and purpose** – successful organisations play to their strengths and the abilities of their people, products, services and markets. They are aware of their organisation's skills and weaknesses and work with business partner organisations to underpin these. They believe in the diversity of their people and therefore have multiple perspectives and strengths throughout. They have a clear vision which is

communicated effectively and a strategy to achieve it. They ensure everything they do is underpinned by their shared corporate values and they have a clear purpose for what they are doing, thus creating a high performance culture.

3 **Strategy, goals and disciplined use of time** – the company's short term strategy should underpin their long term one. They set goals which are milestones towards their visions and then put into practice their natural skills and abilities and are disciplined in their use of time towards those goals. They free up resources for where they will make the most difference (often creating project teams) and then doggedly pursue their goals. However they also know where to stop and do something else if it is not working. Listen out for those early warning signals of impending disaster. If they can't be stopped then change tack.

4 **Risk taking and action orientated** – they trust their leaders and staff at all levels. Empowerment is fundamental. They have leaders at all levels of the organisation. Their leaders trust their intuition and take calculated risks putting into action their decisions and having the flexibility and adaptability to change along the way as appropriate. The structures, processes and systems are in place to ensure efficiency and standards, but freedom is given to ensure creativity and responsiveness is maintained, allowing change to happen quickly. This will in turn create success and a good financial standing.

5 **Relationships – visibility, perceptions and branding** – trust relationships are key both internally throughout the organisation and also externally with stakeholders, partners and clients. You need people to achieve your visions. Successful organisations know the importance of understanding who they are and what they stand for – this is their unique brand. They also realise they need visibility for their great work and manage the perceptions of others. Therefore their internal brand (seen by their staff) and their external brand (client facing) are aligned and they live the brand in everything they do. They have a corporate conscience and balance environmental issues with profit.

6 Leaders who are learners – successful organisations turn any situation to their advantage. Great leaders are given the authority and resources to lead their organisation in the way they see fit. They constantly learn and evolve successfully because of this. They are often known for being lucky – the truth is they are lucky because they analyse what's going on and turn a situation to their advantage.

7 Their People – successful companies focus on aligning happiness and success. They champion well-being and employ rounded whole people that are not just the sum of their role or work but so much more. They encourage work-life balance and are aware of the benefits in performance that brings. A happy worker is a productive worker – no one wants to be the one to let the side down in a workplace like this.

There they are – seven small steps. Easy to learn but will you put them into practise? That's where the really important part starts.

One more time then – turn this into a memory chain and use it when strategic decisions come your way.

"Only those who dare to fail greatly can ever achieve greatly"
Robert F Kennedy –
politician

Appendix One

Here is an alphabet of quick tips for living a successful life:

A lways be proactive, don't wait for opportunities to come to you, go and look for them

B e the person you always wanted to be. No one is stopping you – except you yourself.

C are about others and not only about yourself. They will reciprocate.

D reams are what keep people striving for success.

E nvying the possessions of others is a barrier to getting these things yourself.

F inding yourself in a rut should be your cue to work out how to climb out.

G iving up is not an option – problems are hardly ever insurmountable if you give them some thought.

H ave a good reputation and dress in a way that reflects this.

I nspiration is everywhere – no one ever said that work had to be serious.

J ump on new projects – never wait to be pushed.

K icking a member of staff who gets something wrong or offers a bad suggestion will ensure they never offer you help in the future. Go for constructive criticism.

L eaps of faith often lead to the greatest successes – take well-calculated risks. Life's too short not to.

M entioning buzz words and jargon will make you look an utter prat. *No one* thinks this is big and clever.

N egative emotions and problems should only be pursued if it's to sort them out. Wallowing in self-pity never helped anyone.

Open your mouth only when asked or if you've taken time to consider what you are going to say.

Potential lies in everyone and that means you too. Don't let anyone ever tell you otherwise.

Quit trying, start complaining. This mantra is for people who deserve nothing in life.

Rest on your laurels. This phrase originates from Julius Caesar and look what happened to him.

Setting people up to fail might benefit you in the short term but they, or someone who sees how you operate, will come back to bite you. It's guaranteed.

Trusting people means they will put their trust in you.

Use all the day, every day to look for what is going well – concentrating on failure will just drag you down.

Valuing nothing unless it is very expensive will lead to a life that is so vacuous, you'll be lucky if you don't implode. Some of the world's greatest assets are free.

Waiting until it's too late means your failure will be no one's fault but your own. If something needs to be done then get up and go and do it.

X press your distrust of people and they will treat you accordingly. Even if they really deserve your suspicion remember the adage: 'Keep your friends close and your enemies closer'.

You are a miracle of nature. The chances of you even being here are astronomically small. Never forget it and don't waste your chance. The most likely thing to be standing in you way is your own fear.

Zoology is a science worth remembering – everyone is different and has different needs. Don't presume everyone thinks the same as you.

Appendix Two

How to play **buzzword bingo:**

1. Print this page
2. Take it to your next meeting
3. Listen attentively
4. Collect either pre-chosen terms or just try to fill the chart as they come out
5. Yell "BINGO!" and you're a winner!

Empower [ment]	Mind share	Think outside the box	Best practice	Paradigm
Revisit	Strategic fit	Proactive	Out of the loop	Raise the bar
24/7	Ball park	Game plan	Client focus[ed]	Development opportunity

Here's an empty card for you to copy and start your own games. To make it easier to fit in some of the longer and more delightful terms (e.g. "Are we all singing from the same hymn sheet?") some boxes are bigger than others:

Appendix Three

Chevy Nova Awards – the importance of understanding cultural differences.

Always keen on research the professors came across the following website http://www.greaterthings.com/Humor/chevy_nova.htm

The website lists the nominees for the Chevy Nova Award. Apparently they are given out in honour of GM's fiasco in trying to market this car in Central and South America. "No va" means, of course, "it doesn't go" in Spanish. Now it turns out this was an urban myth and the vehicle sold a large number in South America, but it seemingly led to the awards so something good came out of it. Here are some of the highlights from the website's Rich Kuchinsky:

Coors put its slogan, "Turn It Loose," into Spanish, where it was read as "Suffer From Diarrhea."

Scandinavian vacuum manufacturer Electrolux used the following in an American campaign: "Nothing sucks like an Electrolux."

Clairol introduced the "Mist Stick," a curling iron, into Germany only to find out that "mist" is slang for manure. Not too many people had use for the "Manure Stick."

Colgate introduced a toothpaste in France called Cue, the name of a notorious porno magazine.

An American t-shirt maker in Miami printed shirts for the Spanish market which promoted the Pope's visit. Instead of "I saw the Pope" (el Papa), the shirts read "I Saw the Potato" (la papa).

When Parker Pen marketed a ball-point pen in Mexico, its ads were supposed to have read, "It won't leak in your pocket and embarrass you". The company thought that the word "embarazar" (to impregnate) meant to embarrass, so the ad read: "It won't leak in your pocket and make you pregnant!"

When American Airlines wanted to advertise its new leather first class seats in the Mexican market, it translated its "Fly In Leather" campaign literally, which meant "Fly Naked" (vuela en cuero) in Spanish!

Books that have inspired "The Five Minute Failure". Alternatively if you are really keen please treat this as a reading list.

Alger H Ragged Dick and Mark, *The Match Boy*, New York: Macmillian 1962

Allen, David, *Getting Things Done: The Art of Stress-Free Productivity*, New York Viking, 2001.

Allen, J. *As You Think*, CA: New World Library. 1998

Annunzio, Susan. *Evolutionary Leadership*, Fireside, 2001

Arkana, Penuin. *A Course in Miracles*. 1975

Aron, Elaine N, *The Highly Sensitive Person's Workbook*, Broadway Books, 1999

Assaraf, John, *The Street Kids' Guide to Having It All*, San Diego, 2003

Bailey, Covert, *Ultimate Fit or Fat*, Boston: Houghton Mifflin Company, 2000.

Battalia, O.W. and Tarraut, J.J. *The Corporate Eunuch*, Crowell, 1973

Beck, M. *Finding Your Own North Star*, London: Piatkus. 2001

Bennett, John L. *Leading the Edge of Change*, Paw Print Press, 2000

Bennis, W. *On Becoming a Leader*, London: Arrow. 1989

Berke, Diane. *Love Always Answers*, Crossroads, 1994

Berke, Diane. *The Gentle Smile*, Crossroads, 1994

Berman Fortgang, Laura. *Take Yourself to the Top*, Thorsons, 1998

Bettger, F. *How I Raised Myself from Failure to Success in Selling*, New York: Fireside 1992

Blanchard, K & Johnson S., *The One Minute Manager*, London: HarperCollins 1981

Bliss, C. *Doing It Now*, New York: Macmillan, 1983.

Boddisy, Larry, and Ron Charan. *Execution: The Discipline of Getting Things Done*, New York: Crown Business, 2002

Bohm, David, *Wholeness and the Implicate Order*, Routledge Classics, 2002

Bok, E. W., *The Americanization for Edward Bok: The Autobiography of a Dutch Boy Fifty Years After*, New York: Charles Scribner's Sons 1921

Branden, Nathaniel, *The Six Pillars of Self-Esteem*, New York: Bantam, 1994

Braun, Thom. *The Philosophy of Branding*. Kogan Page 2004

Breathnach, Sarah Ban, *Something More: Excavating Your Authentic Self*, Time Warner International, 2000.

Bridges, W. *Transitions: Making Sense of Life's Changes*. London: Nicholas Brealey Publishing. 1996

Bristol, C. M. *The Magic of Believing*, New York: Simon & Schuster 1949

Brown, Les, *It's Not Over until You Win*, New York: Simon & Schuster, 1997.

Brown, Molly Young, *Growing Whole: Self-Realization on an Endangered Planet*, HarperCollins, 1993

Buchanan and Huczynski, *Organisational Behaviour*, Prentice hall, 1991

Buckingham, Marcus and Donald O. Clifton, *Now Discover Your Strengths*, Audio, 2001

Burns, D. *Feeling Good: The New Mood Therapy*, New York: Avon Books 1992

Butler-Bowdon, Tom. *50 Success Classics*, Maine: Nicholas Brealey Publishing, 2004

Butler-Bowdon, Tom. *50 Self-Help Classics*, Nicholas Brealey, 2003

Byron, Kate. *Loving What Is: Four Questions That Can Change Your Life*, New York: Harmony Books, 2002

Campbell, J. with Moyers, B. *The Power of Myth*, New York: Anchor Books. 1991

Canfield, Jack and Mark Victor Hansen. *Chicken and Soup for the Soul*, 1993.

Canfield, Jack with Janet Switzer. *The Success Principles*, Harper Collins Publishers, 2005

Canfield, Jack and Mark Victor Hansen, *The Aladdin Factor: How to Ask for and Get Anything You Want in Life*, New York: Berkley, 1995.

Carlson R., *Don't Sweat The Small Stuff... And It's All Small Stuff: Simple Ways to Keep the Little things from Overtaking Your Life*, London: Hodder & Stoughton. 1997

Carnegie, D., *How to Win Friends and Influence People*, New York: Pocket Books 1994

Carnegie, A. *The Autobiography of Andrew Carnegie*, Boston: Northeastern University Press, 1986

Carpenter, Tom. *Dialogue on Awakening.* Carpenter Press, 1992.

Charvet, Shelle Rose, *Words the Change Minds*, Kendall/Hunt Publishing, 1995

Chopra, Deepak. *The Seven Spiritual Laws of Success.* New World Library, 1994.

Chu, C-N, *Thick Face, Black Heart: The Asian Path to Thriving, Winning and Succeeding*, London: Nicholas Brealey Publishing 1992

Clason, G., *The Richest Man in Babylon*, London: Plume 1955

Coelho, Paulo. *The Alchemist: A Fable about Following Your Dream.* HarperCollins, 1995

Cohen, Alan. *A deep Breath of Life: Daily Inspiration for Heart centred Living.* Hay House, 1996.

Cohen, Alan. *Joy Is My Compass: Taking the Risk to Follow Your Bliss.* Hay House, 1996.

Colclough, Beechy and Colclough, Josephine. *A Challenge to Change.* Thorsons, 1999.

Colclough, Beechy and Colclough, Josephine. *Get Up and Do it! – Essential Steps to Achieve Your Goal.* BBC Consumer Publishing, 2004.

Collier, R., *The Secret of the Ages*, Oak Harbour, WA: Robert Collier Publications. 1999

Collings, Jim, *Built to Last: The Successful Habits of Visionary Companies*. New York: HarperBusiness, 1997

Collins, Jim., *Good to Great: Why Some Companies Make the Leap... and Others Don't*, London: Random House. 2001

Coonradt, Charles A, *Scorekeeping for Success*, Park City, Utah: Game of Work, 1999.

Coonradt, Charles A, *The Game of Work:How to Enjoy Work as Much as Play*, Park City, Utah: Game of Work 1997

Covey, Stephen. *The 7 Habits of Highly Effective People*. Simon & Schuster, 1989.

Covey, Stephen R, *The 8th Habit*, Audio Franklin Covey 2005

Csikszentmihalyi, M. *Flow: The Psychology of Optimal Experience*, New York: Harper Perennial 1991

Davis, Mark Professor, *Test Your EQ*, Piatkus Books, 2004

De Bono, Edward. *I am right you are wrong*. Penguin books 1991

Deerfield Beach, Fla: *Living Your Dreams*, Health Communications, 2003.

Deering, Dilts and Russell, *Alpha Leadership*, John Wiley and Sons Ltd, 2002

Dell, M with Fredman, C Direct from Dell: *Strategies that Revoluntionized an Industry*, London: HarperBusiness. 1999

DeLuca, Fred and John B Hayes, *Start Small, Finish Big: Fifteen Key Lessons to Start-and Run-Your Own Successful Business*, New York: Warner Books, 2000

Dhammapada: *The Path of Perfection* J. Mascaro, London: Penguin Classics. 1973

Dorner, Dietrich, *The Logic of Failure*, Metropolitan Books, 1996

Drummond, Norman. *The Spirit of Success*, Hodder and Stoughton, 2004

Dwoskin, Sedona, *Ariz, The Sedona Method: Your Key to Lasting Hapiness, Success, Peace and Emotional Well-being*, Sedona Press, 2003

Dyer, W., *Real Magic: Creating Miracles in Everyday Life*, New York: Harper Collins 1993

Einstein, Albert. *The World as I See it.* Editied by Alan Harris, Citadel Press, 1979.

Emerson, R.W. *Self-Reliance and Other Essays*, Dover Publications 1993

Emmett, Rita, *The Procrastinators Handbook: Mastering the Art of Doing it Now*, New York Walker Publishing, 2000

Estes, C.P. *Women Who Run With the Wolves*, London Rider 1993

Etzioni, Amitai. *The Spirit of Community.* HarperCollins, 1995.

Faulkner, Andreas, S, *NLP: The New Technology of Achievement*, London: Nicholas Brealey Publishing 1996

Ford, H., *My Life and Work*, Manchester, NH: Ayer Co. Publishing 1996

Foster Russell and Kreitzman; *The Rhythms of life*, Profile books 2004

Franklin, B., *Autobiography and Other Writings*: Oxford University Press 1993

Franklin, Victor. *Man's Search for Meaning.* Washington Square Press, 1984.

French, Wendell and Cecil H Bell, JR, *Organisation Development*, Prentice-Hall, 1995

Fromm, Erich. *The Art of Being.* Constable & Robinson, 1993.

Fromm, Erich. *To Have or To Be?* Abacus, 1987.

Fromm, Erich. *The Sane Society.* Routledge Classics, 2001.

Galloway, Timothy, *The Inner Game of Work*, Orion Business, 2000

Gallup, George. *The People's Religion: America's Faith in the 90s.* Macmillan, 1990

Garfield, Charles and William Morrow, *Peak Performers: The New Hero's of American Business*, 1986

Gawain, G., *Creative Visualisation*, New York: Bantam Books 1985

Gibran, Kahlil. *The Prophet*. Arrow, 2000

Gelb, Michael. *How To Think like Leonardo da Vinci*, HarperCollins, 1998.

Gerber, Michael, *E-Myth Mastery: The Seven Essential Disciplines for Building a World Class Company*, New York: Harper Business, 2004

Gerber, Michael, *The E-Myth Revisited: Why Most Small Business Don't Work and What to Do About it*, New York, Ivy Books, 1998

Gerber, R., *Leadership the Eleanor Roosevelt Way: Timeless Strategies from the First Lady of Courage*, New York: Prentice Hall, 2002

Gerstner, Louis V JR, *Who Says Elephants Cant Dance? Inside IBM's Historic Turnaround*, New York: HarperBusiness, 2002

Geus, Arie de. *The Living Company: Growth, Learning and Longevity in Business*. Nicholas Brealey Publishing Ltd., 1999.

Giblin, L., *How to Have Confidence and Power in Dealing with People*, New Jersey: Prentice Hall 1956

Gillibrand, Eileen and Mosley, Jenny. *She Who Dares Wins*. Thorsons, 1995.

Gladwell, Malcolm: *The Tipping Point*, Abacus 2002

Gleick, James. *Faster – The Acceleration of Just About Everything*. Abacus, 2000

Godin, Seth. *Purple Cow*, Michael Joseph 2004

Goldratt, Eliyahu M, *The Goal: A Process of Ongoing Improvement* Great Barrington, Mass: North River Press, 1992

Goldsmith, Lyons and Freas, *Coaching for Leadership*, Jossey-Bass/Pfeiffer, 2000

Goleman, Daniel,. *Emotional Intelligence: Why It Can Matter More Than IQ*. Bantam, 1995.

Goleman, Daniel, *Emotional Intelligence*, Bloomsbury, 1996

Gracian, B., *The Art of Worldly Wisdom: A Pocket Oracle*, New York: Currency 1992

Grant, Suzie, *48 hours to a healthier life*: Penguin books 2003

Graves, E.G., *How to Succeed in Business without Being White: Straight Talk on Making It in America*, New York: HarperCollins 1977

Gray, John, *The Mars and Venus Diet and Exercise Solution*, PhD New York: St Martin's Press, 2003

Gray, J., *Men are from Mars, Women are from Venue: A Practical Guide for Improving Communication and Getting What You Want in Your Relationships*, London: HarperCollins 1992

Greene, Robert and Joost Elffers, *48 Laws of Power*, Profile Books 1998,

Hall, Richard, *Success*, Pearson Education, 2005

Handy, Charles and Elizabeth: *The New Alchemists*: Hutchinson 2004

Harnish, Verne, *Mastering the Rockefeller Habits*, New York: Select Books, 2002

Harvard Business review, *Breakthrough Leadership*, 2001

Harvey, Joan and Katz, Cynthia. *If I'm so Successful Why Do I Feel Like a Fake? The Imposter Syndrome*. St. Martin's Press, 1985.

Hawkins, David, R, M.D Carlsbad, *Power vs Force: The Hidden Determinants of Human Behavior*, Calif: Hay House, 2002

Hay, Julie, *Dealing with Difficult People*, Audio

Hay, L (1999) *You Can Heal Yourself*, Carlsbad CA: Hay House

Heppell, Michael. *How to Be Brilliant*, Pearson Prentice Hall, 2004

Hicks, Esther and Jerry, *Ask and It Is Given: Learning to Manifest Your Desires*. Carlsbad, Calif: Hay House, 2004

Higgs, M Dr and Dulewicz, V Prof, *Making Sense of Emotional Intelligence*, Nfer-Nelson, 1999

Hill, N & Stone, W.C *Success through a Positive Mental Attitude*, London:Thorsons 1990

Hill, N., *Think and Grow Rich*, New York: Fawcett Crest 1960

Hillman, J., *The Souls Code: In Search of Character and Calling*, New York: Warner Books 1997

His Holiness the Dalai Lama & Howard C. Cutler., *The Art of Happiness: A Handbook for Living*, London: Hodder & Stroughton 1999

Holden, Robert. *Happiness NOW!* Hodder & Stoughton, 1998.

Holden, Robert. *Hello Happiness*. Hodder & Stoughton, 1999.

Holden, Robert. *Stress Busters*. HarperCollins, 1992.

Holden, Robert, *Success Intelligence*, Hodder and Stoughton, 2005

Holden, Robert. *Laughter, The Best Medicine*. HarperCollins, 1993.

Hooper, Alan and Potter, John. *Intelligent Leadership: Creating the Habit of Excellence*. Random House, 2000.

Hopkins, T., *The Official Guide to Success*, W. Jamison HarperCollins 1993

James, M. & Jongeward, D., *Born to Win: Transactional Analysis with Gestalt Experiments*, New York: Perseus Books 1996

James, Oliver. *Britain on the Couch – Why We're Unhappier than We Were in the 1950s – Despite Being Richer*. Century Books, 1997.

James, William. *The Principles of Psychology*. Harvard University Press, 1990.

Jaworski, Joseph. *Synchronicity – The Inner Path of Leadership*. Berrett – Koehler, 1996.

Jay, Mike, *Coach 2 the Bottom Line*, Trafford Publishing, 1999

Jeffers, Susan. *End the Struggle and Dance with Life*. Hodder & Stoughton, 1996

Jeffers, Susan. *Feel the Fear and Do it Anyway*. Rider, 1991.

Johnson, Spencer Dr, *Who Moves My Cheese*, Penguin Putnam, 1998

Jorge Cruise, *8 Minutes in the Morning*, by New York: HarperCollins, 2001

Jung, Carl. *Synchronicity: An Acausal Connecting Principle.* Princeton University Press, 1969.

Kennedy, Carol, *From Dynasties to Dotcoms*, Kogan Page, 2003

Kimbro, P, *Think and Grow Rich: A Black Choice*, 1997

King, Peter J, *One Hundred Philosophers*, Quarto Publishing Plc, 2004

Kiyosaki, R with Lechter, S., *Rich Dad, Poor Dad: What the Rich Teach Their Kids about Money...That the Poor and Middle Class Do Not!* London: Time Warner 1997

Koch, T., *The 80/20 Principle: The Secret of Achieving More with Less*, London: Nicholas Brealey Publishing 1998

Lambert, Tom, *High Income Consulting*, Nicholas Brealey Publishing, 1997

Landes, D.S., *The Wealth and Poverty of Nations: Why Some are so Rich and Some are so Poor*, Abacus 1998

Landsberg, Max, *The Tao of Coaching*, Harper Collins, 1997

Langer, E., *Mindfulness: Choice and Control in Everyday Life*, Cambridge, MA: Perseus Publishing 1990

Lao-Tzu Tao Te Ching trans. T Freke, London: Piatkus 2000

Lasch, Christopher. *The Culture of Narcissism.* W.W. Norton & Co, 1979.

Lazear, Jonathon. *Meditations for Men Who Do Too Much.* Thorsons, 1992.

Leider, Richard J, *The power of purpose*, Berrett-Koehler publishers

Lencioni, Patrick., *Five Dysfunctions of a team.* Jossey Bass Wiley 2002

Lencioni, Patrick M, *The Five Temptations of a CEO: A Leadership Fable*, San Francisco: Jossey-Bass, 1998

Leonard, J Thomas, *The Portable Coach*, Simon and Schuster, 1998

Linder, Steffan. *The Harried Leisure Class*. Columbia University Press, 1969.

Loehr, J. & Schwartz, T., *On Form*, Nicholas Brealey Publishing 2003

Lowenstein, R. Buffett., *The Making of an American Capitalist*, London: Orion 1995

Lowndes, Leil. *How to Talk to anyone*, HarperCollins Publishing, 2003

Lynch, James. *The Broken Heart*. Hodder & Stoughton, 1997.

Maitland, Iain, *Motivating People*, Training Extras, 1995

Maltz, Maxwell. *Psycho-Cybernetics*. Prentice-Hall, 1960.

Mandela, N.R., *Long Walk to Freedom: The Autobiography of Nelson Mandela*, London: Abacus 1994

Mandino, Og. *Secrets of Success and Happiness*. Ballantine Bokks, 1995.

Manz, Charles C. *The Power of Failure*, Berrett-Koehler, 2002

Marden, O.S., *Pushing to the Front, or Success under difficulties*, Vols 1 & 2 Santa Fe CA: Sun Books 1997

Marriott, J.W. Jr with Brown, K.A., *The Spirit to Serve: Marriott's Way*, New York: HarperCollins 1997

Maslow, A., *Motivation and Personality*, ed. R. Frager, New York: Addison Wesley 1987

Mascaro, J., *The Bhagavad-Gita* London: Penguin World's Classics. 1973

McGraw, P., *Life Strategies: Doing What Works, Doing What Matters*, London: Vermillion 2001

McKeith, Gillian D.R., *You are What you Eat*, Penguin Books, 2004

Meyer, M, Thoreau, H.D., *Walden and Civil Disobedience*, New York: Penguin 1986

Moody, Raymond A, *Life After Life*, Jr M.D. New York: Bantam, 1994

Moore, T., *Care of the Soul*, New York: HarperCollins 1992

Morrell, M. & Capparell, S., *Shackleton's Way: Leadership Lesson from the Great Antarctic Explorer*, Nicholas Brealey Publishing 2001

Muller, Wayne. *Legacy of the Heart*. Hodder & Stoughton, 1997.

Murphy, J., *The Power of Your Subconscious Mind*, London: Pocket Books 1995

Myers, David. *The American Paradox: Spiritual Hunger in an Age of Plenty*. Yale University Press, 2000.

Myers, David. *The Pursuit of Happiness – Discovering the Pathway to Fulfillment, Well-being and Enduring and Personal Joy*. Avon Books, 1993.

Nelson, Bob. *1001 Ways to Reward Employees*, New York: Workman Publishing, 1994

O'Connor Joseph, *NLP & Sports*, Thorsons, 2001

O'Connor, Joseph, *NLP Workbook*, Thorsons, 2001

O'Connor Joseph and Robin Prior. *Success Selling with NLP*, Thorsons, 1995

O'Neill, John R. *The Paradox of Success: When Winning at Work Means Losing at Life*. J.P. Tarcher, 1994.

Ornish, Dean. *Love and Survival – 8 Pathways to Intimacy and Health*. HarperPerrenial, 1998.

Panzer, Richard. *Relationship Intelligence*. Center for Educational Media, 1999.

Peale, N.V. (1996) *The Power of Positive Thinking*, New York: Ballantine Books

Pearman, Roger R, *Hard Wired Leadership*, Davies Black Publishing, 1998

Pearsall, Paul. *Toxic Success: How to Avoid Striving and Start Thriving*. Inner Ocean Publishing, 2002.

Pearson, C., *The Hero Within*, San Francisico, CA: HarperCollins 1998

Pease, Allan and Barbara. *Why Men Don't Listen and Why Women Cant Read Maps*. Orion Books, 1999

Peck, M.S., *The Road Less Travelled: A New Psychology of Love, Traditional Valurs and Spiritual Growth*, London: Arrow Books 1990

Peters, Tom and Robert Waterman. *In Search of Excellence: Lessons from America's Best-Run Companies*. HarperCollins, 1982.

Peters Tom, *Re-imagine:* Dorling Kindersley 2003

Peters, Tom. The Circle of Innovation. Hodder & Stoughton, 1997.

Peterson, David, B, *Leader as Coach*, Personnel Decisions International, 1996

Pfeffer, Jeffrey, *The Human Equation*, Harvard Business School Press, 1998

Phillips, Bill, *Body for Lie: 12 Weeks to Mental and Spiritual Strength*, New York Harper-Collins, 1999

Phillips, D.T., *Lincoln on Leadership: Executive Strategies for Tough Times*, New York: Warner Books 1992

Ponder, C., *The Dynamic Laws of Prosperity*, Camarillo, CA: DeVorss & Co. 1962

Popcorn, Faith. *The Popcorn Report – Targetting Your Life*. Arrow Books, 1992.

Porter, Michael., *Competitive Strategy*. Free Press 2004

Proctor, Bob, *You Were Born Rich*, Willowdale, Ontario, Canada 1984

Q Learning, *Motivator*, Book Point Limited, 2003

Q Learning, *Leader*, Book Point Limited, 2003

Rand, A., *Atlas Shrugged*, New York: Signet Books 1996

Riesman, David. *The Lonely Crowd*. Revised Edition. Yale Nota Bene, 2001.

Redfield, James and Carol Adrienne, *The Celestine Prophecy*, Bantam Books, 1995

Reese, Maryann, *Sorting Styles*, Marshall University, Video, 1990

Renshaw, Ben. *Successful but Something Missing*. Rider, 2000.

Renshaw, Ben and Alexander, Graham. *Super Coaching – The Missing Ingredient for High Performance*. Dorling Kindersley, 2005.

Renshaw, Ben. *Together but Something Missing*. Rider, 2001.

Richardson, C., *Take Time for Your Life: A Seven Step Programme for Creating the Life You Want*, Bantam : 1998

Risner, Nigel, *It's a Zoo around Here*, Limitless Publications, 2003

Roazzi, Vincent, M, *The Spirituality of Success: Getting Rich with Integrit*, Dallas: Brown Books, 2002.

Robbins, A., *Awaken the Giant Within*, New York: Simon & Schuster, 1993

Robbins, Anthony. *Unlimited Power*. Simon & Schuster, 1988.

Robey, Dan, *The Power of Positive Habits*, Miami: Abritt Publishing

Roddickm Anita. *Business as Unusual*. Thorsons, 2000.

Rollinson, Broadfield and Edwards, *Organisational Behaviour and Analysis*, Addison-Wesley, Longman, 1998

Ruettiger, Rudy, Mike Celizic. Dallas, *Tex: Rudy's Rules for Success*, Tex: Doddridge Press, 1995.

Ruiz, Don Miguel, *The Four Agreement: A Practical Guide to Personal Freedom*, San Rafael: Amber-Allen, 1999.

Sandage, Scott, *Born Losers*, Harvard University Press, 2005

Sartwell, Matthew, *Napoleon Hill's Key to Success: The 17 Principles of Personal Achievement*. New York: Plume 1997

Schwarts, D.J., *The Magic of Thinking Big*, New York: Simons & Schuster 1959

Schwart, Jim Loehr and Tony, *The Power of Full Engagement*, New York: Free Press, 2002.

Scitovsky, Tibor. *The Joyless Economy*. Oxford University Press, 1976.

Scovell Shinn, F., *The Secret Door to Success*, Camarillo, CA: De Vorss & Co 1978

Scovell Shinn, F., *The Game of Life and How to Play it*, Saffron Walden: C.W. Daniel, 1998

Seligman, M., *Learned Optimism*, New York: Simon & Schuster 1998

Seligman, Marti. *Authentic Happiness*. The Free Press, 2002.

Senge, Kleiner, Roberts, Ross and Smith, *The Fifth Discipline*, Nicholas Brealey Publishing, 1994

Shiller, Robert J. *Irrational Exuberance*. Princeton University Press, 2001.

Smith, Hyrum, W, *The 10 Natural Laws of Successful Time and Life Management: Proven Strategies for Increased Productivity and Inner Peace*, New York 1994

Spezzano, Chuck. *50 Ways To Let Go and Be Happy*. Hodder & Stoughton, 2001.

Stanley, T.J., *The Millionaire Mind*, Sydney: HarperCollins 2000

Stone, Clement, *The Success System That Never Fails, Sun Tzu The Art of War*, Denma Translation Group, Boston: Shambhala 2002

Tam, Marily, *How to Use What You've Got to Get and What You Want*, San Diego 2003

Templar, Richard. *The Rules of Work*, Prentice Hall, 2003

The Dhammapada: *Saying of Buddha*, T.F. Cleary, New York: HarperCollins 1995

The Mind Gym, *Wake up your mind*, Time Warner Books, 2005

The Mind Gym, *Give me time*, Time Warner Books, 2006

Tolle, Eckhart, *The Power of Now: A guide to Spiritual Enlightenment*, Novato, Calif: New World Library, 1999.

Tracy, B, *Create Your Own Future*, New York: John Wiley & Sons

Tracy, B, *The 100 Absolutely Unbreakable Laws of Business Success*, Berret-Koehler, 2000

Tracy, B, *Maximum Achievement: Strategies and Skills that Will Unlock Your Hidden Powers to Succeed*, New York: Fireside 1993

Trine, Ralph. Waldo. *In Tune with the Infinite*. HarperCollins, 2001.

Trump, Donald; *Trump - How to get rich*; BBC consumer publishing, 2004

Turner, Suzanne: *Tools for Success*, McGraw-Hill 2003

Van Maurik, John. *The Effective Strategist*, Gower, 1999

Van Maurik, John. *Writers on Leadership*, Penguin, 2001

Vasari, Giorgio. *The Lives of the Artists*. Oxford University Press, 1998.

Wallace, William. *Michelangelo – The Complete Sculpture, Painting*, Architecture. Hugh Lauter Levin Associates, 1998.

Walton, S with Huey, J., *Made in America: My Story*, New York: Bantam 1992

Wattles, W.D., *Financial Success through the Power of Thought (The Science of Getting Rich)*, Rochester, Vermont: Destiny Books 1976

Webster, Adrian, *Polar Bear Pirates*, Capstone Publishing Ltd, 2002

Welch, Jack, *Straight from the Guy*, New York: Warner, 2001

Welch, J with Byrne, J Jack: *What I've Learned Leading a Great Company and Great People*, Headline 2001

White, John. *What is Enlightenment?* Aquarian Press, 1998.

Whitmore, J., *Coaching for Performance: GROWing People, Performance and Purpose*, London: Nicholas Brealey Publishing 1992

White, Jennifer, *Work Less, Make More*, New York: John Wiley & Sons

Whyte, David. *The Heart Aroused.* The Industrial Society, 1997.

Williams, A.L., *All You Can Do IS All You Can Do But All You Can Do Is Enough!* New York: Ivy Books, 1998

Williams, Jay, *The 24-Hour Turnaround: The Formula for Permanent Weight Loss, Antiaging and Optimal Health – Starting Today!* New York: Regan Books, 2002

Williamson, Marianne. *A Return of Love.* Thorsons, 1992.

Williams, Nick. *The Work We Were Born To Do.* Element, 2000.

Williams, Nick. *Powerful Beyond Measure.* Bantam Press, 2003.

Williams, Nick. *Unconditional Success*, Bantam Press, 2002.

Wilson, Larry, *Play to Win: Choosing Growth Over Fear in Work and Life*,

Wilson, Paul. *Calm for Life*, Penguin, 2000.

Wiseman, R., *The Luck Factor: Change Your Luck – And Change Your Life*, Century 2003

Wood, Andrew and Brian Tracy, *The Traits of Champions: The Secrets to Championship Performance in Business Life*, Provo, Utah: Executive Excellence Publishing 2000

Woodward, Clive, *Winning*, Hodder and Stoughton , 2004

Young, Steve. *Great Failures of the Extremely Successful*, Tallfellow Press, 2002

Zander, Rosamund Stone and Benjamin Zander., *The Art of Possibility: Transforming Personal and Professional Life*, New York: Penguin, 2000.

Ziglar, Z., *See You at the Top: 25th Anniversary Edition*, Gretna, LA: Pelican Publishing 2000

Zohar, Danah. *Rewiring the Corporate Brain*. Berrett-Koehler, 1997.

Zohar, Danah and Marshall, Ian. *Spiritual Intelligence – The Ultimate Intelligence*. Bloomsbury, 2000.

Zohar, Danah and Marshall, Ian. *Spiritual Capital*. Berrett-Koehler, 2004.

Zohar, Danah. *The Quantum Self*. Bloomsbury, 1990.

Zohar, Danah and Marshall, Ian. *The Quantum Society*. Bloomsbury, 1994.

www.collegeoffailure.com